The Memoirs of
Margaret S. Mahler

Margaret Mahler in adolescence. *(From the Estate of Margaret S. Mahler.)*

The Memoirs of Margaret S. Mahler

Compiled and Edited by
Paul E. Stepansky

THE FREE PRESS
A Division of Macmillan, Inc.
NEW YORK

Collier Macmillan Publishers
LONDON

The Free Press
A Division of Macmillan, Inc.
866 Third Avenue, New York, N.Y. 10022

Collier Macmillan Canada, Inc.

Printed in the United States of America

printing number
1 2 3 4 5 6 7 8 9 10

Library of Congress Cataloging-in-Publication Data

Mahler, Margaret S.
  The memoirs of Margaret S. Mahler.

  Bibliography: p.
  Includes index.
  1. Mahler, Margaret S.   2. Psychoanalysts—
Biography.   3. Infant psychology.   4. Child
analysis.   I. Stepansky, Paul E.   II. Title.
BF719.M34 1988   154.4'092'4 [B] 88–1199
ISBN 0–02–931260–4

Contents

Acknowledgments

The preparation of Margaret Mahler's memoirs for posthumous publication was undertaken at the request of, and with the full cooperation of, the executors of Dr. Mahler's estate, Mrs. Bernice Apter, Bernard Fischman, Esq., and Maria Nardone, Ph.D. It has been a pleasure working with the executors, and I thank them warmly for their unstinting support of this project, which included giving me complete freedom to organize and present as I saw fit the interview transcript material from which the memoirs derive. Special thanks go to Dr. Nardone for her efforts in amassing these various transcripts and the collateral materials made available to me. The Margaret S. Mahler Psychiatric Research Foundation has also been supportive of my preparation of the memoirs, and it is a pleasure to acknowledge the foundation's important role in furthering Dr. Mahler's work.

Dr. Doris Nagel functioned as my critical reader during the preparation of the memoirs; she has my deep gratitude for many thoughtful suggestions that enabled me to fine-tune the manuscript. Five of Dr. Mahler's colleagues were likewise kind enough to read memoir chapters as they were drafted. I thank Dr. Peter Blos, Dr. Judith Kestenberg, Dr. Selma Kramer, Dr. Peter

Neubauer, and especially Dr. Annemarie Weil for helpful comments that enabled me, on Dr. Mahler's behalf, to ascertain correctly certain matters of fact. Finally, I thank Dr. Nagel, Dr. Kramer, Dr. Weil, and Dr. John McDevitt for helpful comments on that section of my introductory essay summarizing Dr. Mahler's work; I assume full responsibility for these remarks, knowing full well that these colleagues of Dr. Mahler's would not have summarized her work exactly as I have.

Dr. Nardone, Dr. Weil, Dr. Blos, Dr. Kramer, and Dr. Irving Sternschein have expedited my work on the photo inserts contained in these memoirs, especially helping me ascertain the contexts and dates of the more recent photos contained in the second insert. Nanci Young, an archivist at Yale University Library, the repository of Dr. Mahler's papers, was most cooperative in bringing to my attention photos now in the possession of Yale; she was likewise kind enough to consult the Mahler papers, which are not yet available to scholars, in order to help me establish the exact dates of Dr. Mahler's training at the four universities she attended from 1916 to 1922.

Joyce Seltzer of The Free Press has been a supportive and accommodating editor from start to finish. Eleanor Starke Kobrin, my colleague at The Analytic Press, has been an understanding and critically helpful friend. My wife, Deane Rand Stepansky, is my partner in this project. She proofread and commented on preliminary drafts of each chapter, patiently answered a plethora of grammatical, syntactical, and presentational questions, and cheerfully allowed me the many evenings and weekends absorbed by the project. To her, as always, my heartfelt gratitude.

P.E.S.

November 1987

Materials Consulted
in Preparation of *Memoirs*

Interviews (4) of 1969 and 1974 with Dr. Bluma Swerdloff, Oral History Research Office, Columbia University, 117 pp.

Statement submitted by Margaret Mahler to the "Pioneers Panel" at meeting of the International Association for Child Psychiatry and Allied Professions, Philadelphia, August 1, 1974, 9 pp.

Interview with Dr. William Langford, 1970s, videotape.

Interview with Margaret McDonald, New York, 1977, 9pp. Printed in *Psychiatric News,* vol. 12, no. 7, April 1, 1977, pp. 20–21, 30–31.

Interview with Dr. Milton J. E. Senn, New York, December 1, 1977, 25 pp.

Precis of Memoirs of Margaret S. Mahler, prepared by Margaret Mahler and Darlene Levy, n.d., 24 pp.

Interview with Dr. Raquel Berman, New York, July 23, 1979, videotape.

Interview with Dr. Eleanor Galenson, Cascais, Portugal, April 4, 1980, videotape.

Interviews of 1980 and 1981 with Dr. Doris Nagel (intended to be the basis of the Mahler memoirs), New York, 146 pp.

Interview with Dr. Doris Nagel, under title "Autobiography of Dr. M. Mahler, edited by Alexander Schlesinger for Dr. M. Mahler," New York, n.d., 35 pp.

Interview with Dr. Nancy Chodorow, March 26, 1981, New York, 57 pp.

Interview with Dr. Joseph Noshpitz, May 2, 1981, New York, 35 pp.

Interview with Dr. Rose Stein, Hungarian Oral History Project, Oral History Research Office, Columbia University, 1984, 18 pp.

Judith R. Smith, "Margaret S. Mahler, M.D.: Original Thinker, Exceptional Woman," in Leah J. Dickstein and Carol C. Nadelson, eds., *Women Physicians in Leadership Roles*. Washington: American Psychiatric Press, 1986, pp. 111–19.

Eulogies delivered at the funeral of Margaret Mahler by Anni Bergman, Bernard Fischman, Selma Kramer, John McDevitt, and Patricia Nachman, October 6, 1985.

Introduction *by* Paul E. Stepansky

I

When Margaret Schönberger Mahler died in 1985 at the age of 88, colleagues the world over marked the passing of an extraordinary child psychoanalyst who, long accorded the status of a grande dame in her profession, was widely regarded as one of the outstanding students of early childhood development of our century. What was generally lost amid the predictable encomia to a remarkable clinician, researcher, and teacher was the drama of the life she had lived. For Margaret Mahler did not sail to easy eminence across the relatively calm seas of American psychiatry and psychoanalysis. Rather, her achievements and her reputation have as their backdrop more troubled European waters. Confronted in early life with sexism and anti-Semitism, coming of age professionally over the resistance of influential elements of the Viennese psychoanalytic establishment, and making her mark as a researcher and theorist in the aftermath of the wrenching émigré experience of the late thirties, Mahler is remarkable in different ways. It is edifying not only to know the woman, and how much she overcame to accomplish her life's work, but to rehearse with her, in these memoirs, a triumph over adversity that brings into its compass so many crosscurrents of European and American cultural experience.

Born in the provincial Hungarian village of Sopron in 1897, Mahler, in her youth, epitomized the struggle to break loose from bourgeois moorings and achieve professional success that animated many female intellectuals in the early years of the new century. The years of her training in medicine witnessed the ascendency of German fascism. Virulent anti-Semitism dogged her all along the way; the Hungarian *numerus clausus,* the Kapp Putsch, and the arbitrary detention of Jewish students by police were among the realities of her student years. As a practicing pediatrician and member of the Vienna Psychoanalytic Society, she lived through the erosion of Austrian political life during the twenties and thirties, culminating in the German Anschluss of 1938. Following the Anschluss, she joined the legion of Jewish intellectuals and professionals—the émigrés—who fled Austria and Germany. After a brief sojourn in London, she came to America, where she weathered the storm of World War II, politically secure but emotionally distraught for those left behind. Her anxieties about family members were well founded; fascism left permanent scars. But in the aftermath of the war, undaunted by personal tragedy, she continued a professional ascent begun in the Old World. Over the course of almost five decades, she became the Margaret Mahler known to infant researchers, psychotherapists, and educators.

The characters who accompanied Margaret Mahler on her personal journey, guiding her, testing her, and occasionally opposing her, are an exalted lot. Sandor Ferenczi, perhaps the most gifted of Freud's original disciples, was her mentor and inspiration. He along with Michael Balint, another of Freud's distinguished Hungarian followers; Geza Roheim, the anthropologist; and Robert Bereney, the painter, were members of the earliest circle of intimates to nourish her intellectually. Their place was taken, some years later, by an even more distinguished coterie revolving around the philosopher Karl Jaspers and including Karl and Julia Mannheim. As a medical student and resident physician, she trained under, and won the esteem—at times grudgingly—of the most distinguished pediatricians in Europe: Rudolph von Degkwitz, Jussuf Ibrahim, Leopold Moll, Bélà Schick, and Clemens von Pirquet. As a psychoanalyst, she was Ferenczi's protégée, but she trained under, and did battle with, the titans of the Vienna Psychoanalytic Society, including Helene Deutsch and Anna Freud. And she reached professional maturity under the tutelage of Austria's most influential pedagogue and student of delinquency and crime: August Aichhorn.

Along the way, Mahler undertook numerous "extracurricular" pursuits, any one of which could easily have been the nucleus of a distinguished career. Even as a medical student, she was handpicked by Rudolph von Degkwitz to aid him in pioneering research on the development of a measles vaccine. As a pediatrics resident in Vienna, she was hired by either R. Fåhraeus or one of his close associates to conduct extensive experiments with starting sedimentation rates; Fåhraeus, it will be recalled, was the Swedish researcher who developed this laboratory technique after World War I. She also measured the tonsils of several thousand Viennese school children for von Pirquet, whose findings on the indiscriminate removal of tonsils led to the abandonment of routine tonsillectomy in both Europe and the United States. And she found time, several years later, to become a recognized expert on the administration and interpretation of Rorschach tests, trained by no less an authority than Behn-Eschenburg, a Swiss pupil of Rorschach himself. But these impressive achievements, including her promising career in clinical pediatrics, are preliminaries. They testify to her wide-ranging talents and allude to the drive and ambition that infused the period of her training. But they give little sense of her professional resting place, of the child psychoanalyst she would become and of the psychoanalytically inspired research she would conduct.

II

Among students of child development, educators, and mental health workers of all stripes and colors, Margaret Mahler is best known as the author of *The Psychological Birth of the Human Infant* (1975), a groundbreaking study of the developmental process by which human infants become psychological human beings— the process, that is, by which infants grow into children with an autonomy and individuality bespeaking self-awareness and a capacity for self-reflection. Her seminal findings about early human development have long been gathered within the expression "separation-individuation process," a term that denotes the series of stages marking the infant's gradual intrapsychic "separation" from the mother and correlative understanding of himself as a distinct individual in a world composed of other equally distinct individuals—as an individual, that is, with a subjectively felt sense of identity. Mahler's deepening understanding of the stages comprising the separation-individuation process is chronologically charted in volume II of her *Selected Papers;* in *The Psychological Birth of the Human Infant,* she provides a comprehensive—and eminently accessible—overview that synthesizes over a decade of research.

Many of the insights that have grown out of Mahler's early expositions of the separation-individuation process have not only become part of the professional nomenclature of mental health workers, but entered the everyday lexicon of interpersonal relationships. Consider the term *symbiosis.* To the extent that mental health workers and psychologically astute laymen characterize relationships of extreme dependency as "symbiotic relationships," and speak of the chronic needs of such people for support and reassurance as "symbiotic needs," they operate within a Mahlerian paradigm. It was Mahler who invoked the notion of a "normal symbiotic phase" to characterize the experience of the infant who, shortly after birth, depended on his mother so totally that the two were fused symbiotically. Such dependency was the experiential counterpart of the infant's inability to differentiate himself from the mother. It was owing to this initial state of fusion, this failure on the infant's part to distinguish between "I" and "Not-I," that Mahler was led to construe the infant and mother, jointly, as a "dual unity within one common boundary."[1] In fact, even the condition of symbiosis was, for Mahler, a developmental achievement, since it evolved out of a still earlier "normal autistic phase" in which the newborn infant, existing in a half-sleeping, half-waking state that approximated prenatal existence, was unresponsive to outside stimuli altogether.[2] By observing and describing the devastating consequences of the infant's failure to achieve the first, necessary condition of symbiosis or, having once achieved it, to pass beyond it, she provided a new framework for understanding the major psychological disturbances of childhood that remains influential among psychotherapists and psychoanalysts.

But it was in turning to the "normal" separation-individuation process, whence she observed and explained how the healthy infant grew out of his initial fusion with his mother, that Mahler's work entered the public consciousness in enduring ways. For it was in the context of her interest in the relatively minor trials and tribulations of normal development that she was able to use her research findings prescriptively, suggesting ways in which therapists, teachers, and parents could facilitate the child's passage from dependency to independence, from symbiosis to autonomy. To the extent that psychotherapists, child care workers, educators, and mothers alike have come to appreciate that optimal mothering involves a delicate balance between "holding on" and "letting go"—that children achieve healthy independence and autonomy because healthy mothers let these children move away from them in exploratory and creative ways, even as these same mothers remain available to comfort and soothe (to provide what Mahler terms "emotional refueling"), they appropriate a fundamental insight derived from Mahler's observational research. Therapists and educators who have come to understand that a felt sense of identity—of coherent sameness and integrity across time—is less a fact of life than a hard-won developmental achievement, subject to vicissitudes and pitfalls, likewise incorporate the yield of countless observational studies of the separation-individuation process. Finally, in providing a timetable of the developmental challenges that young children meet, including the obstacles they must overcome in the various "subphases" of the separation-individuation process, she, virtually alone among contemporary psychoanalysts, has extended Freud's legacy into the public domain in constructive and eminently accessible ways. Mothers and teachers unfamiliar with, and otherwise uninterested in, psychoanalysis or alternative "scientific" approaches to childrearing may well know of, and derive considerable benefit from, Mahler's pioneering work.

It is predictable and appropriate that Mahler's concepts and insights should have filtered down to a broad public of educators and parents. Unlike Freud, whose developmental insights revolved around issues of fatherhood, especially as they were implicated in the Oedipus complex, Mahler was among the early psychoanalysts to make the *relationship* between child and mother integral to a psychoanalytically informed appreciation of early development. In so doing, she lent specificity to the injunction of the great Austro-American "ego psychologist" Heinz Hartmann that psychoanalysts supplement Freud's preoccupation with the life of instinct with an attentiveness to "adaptation" and the "average expectable environment" in which adaptation occurs. Mahler realized Hartmann's imperative by making the infant's growth-promoting environment inhere in the specific person of the mother; she was thereupon led to construe adaptation as the product of an interactive fit between a child's needs and his mother's ability and willingness to provide care that addressed these needs. Compared to Hartmann and other ego psychologists, for whom "adaptation" and "environment" were fairly empty generalities, then, Mahler's depiction of the characteristic patterns of infantile need and maternal response constituted, in the words of two recent commentators, "a much more specific and relational view of adaptation to the environment than that of Hartmann's original broadly sketched version."[3]

Now a number of Mahler's contemporaries—some eminent, like Melanie Klein, Erik Erikson, René Spitz, and D. W. Winnicott, others less well known, like Therese Benedek and Mahler's great friend Alice Balint—participated in this same generational thrust by which motherhood came to share center stage with fatherhood in psychoanalytic perspectives on the first years of life. But Mahler, alone among her contemporaries, was not content to "theorize" about the first years of life on the basis of clinical psychoanalytic work with older children and adults. Rather, her clinical experience, both as a pediatrician and as a psychoanalyst, posed questions that could only be addressed, and eventually answered, through observational research in a naturalistic setting.

The history and methodology of the research projects that eventuated in Mahler's understanding of the separation-individuation process are fully described in *The Psychological Birth of the Human Infant* and summarily reviewed in the memoirs. Here let me say only a few prefatory words. In brief, Mahler's projects involved the observing and recording (including filming) of descriptive-clinical data about infants and toddlers, their mothers, and, most especially, the interaction between mothers and their very young offspring. These observations were recorded several times weekly in a natural setting in which the day-to-day relationship between mother and child would, over time, be apparent.

The central phenomenon under study was the infant's and toddler's separation from the mother. Whereas, from the outset, Mahler understood separation-individuation to be an *intrapsychic* process that could not be directly observed, her research was guided by her belief that this process "could be inferred from behaviors that were indeed observable."[4] It is this belief that observable separation experiences are only behavioral reflections of a *psychological* achievement (or its relative absence) that distinguishes Mahler's work from that of the many "attachment" theorists who have also investigated the mother-child relationship over time. Attachment theorists do not understand the infant's and young child's observable attachment to his mother in terms of a developmental agenda, internal to the child, that leads out of attachment to separation and individuation. Rather, they view attachment behavior, which is to say behavior tending toward, and resulting in, a comfortable proximity to the mother, as an evolutionary inheritance that is, per se, instinctive in promoting survival. Separation, psychologically understood, is not programmed into, not the expectable outcome of, attachment. But the *quality* of one's early attachment experiences, according to the attachment theorists, will determine one's subsequent ability to *cope* with the many separations and losses that life brings.

By way of underscoring the psychological and, more specifically, psychoanalytic frame of reference of Mahler's separation-individuation process, it is perhaps worthwhile to pause briefly and consider her approach alongside that of John Bowlby, the greatest of the attachment theorists and, like Mahler, the progenitor of a school of thought and a research program carried on by others. Bowlby, like Mahler, comes to the study of the infant-mother interaction from psychoanalysis, but opts at once for a descriptive approach to this interaction that is, in its essentials, ethological rather than psychological. For Bowlby, that is, the infant's attachment to his mother, including his reactions on being separated from her, is the product of instinctive behavioral systems that promote survival; as such, it can be explained on the model of animal, and especially primate, attachment behavior. Since such behavior often occurs reciprocally between child and mother, and since the stimuli that elicit such behavior are generally *human* stimuli (e.g., the mother's face and voice that draw her infant to her; the infant's cry of loneliness that induces his mother to rock him), Bowlby can speak of attachment behavior as "a class of social behavior," one in which "the child's tie to his mother is a product of the activity of a number of behavioral systems that have proximity to mother as a predictable outcome."[5] Given that the infant's attachment to his mother is predicated upon behaviors that promote nearness to the mother, it follows that attachment behavior only begins when the infant is around six months old, since it is only at this time that "there is evidence that the infant not only recognizes his mother but tends also to behave in a way that maintains his proximity to her.[6]

It is to Bowlby's great credit to have charted the waxing and waning of attachment behavior over the course of childhood, including the child's recourse to various forms of behavior that "mediate" attachment (such as smiling, crying, babbling, clinging, and sucking), the mother's role in promoting (or discouraging) the child's attachment, and the child's responses to experiences of separation and loss. But this descriptively rich approach to such phenomena is far removed from that of Mahler, for whom attachment and separation "experiences" are external analogues to an internal process, which is to say a process that occurs *within* the infant and child, even though it is influenced by what has transpired *between* the child and his mother.[7]

For Bowlby, the toddler's attachment behavior is instinctive, but not in any "species-specific" much less "Freudian" sense; the factors that promote attachment behavior in man, notably protection from predators, "are not greatly different from what they are in his mammalian relatives."[8] Not so for Mahler. The distinctively human condition of "symbiosis," from which separation and individuation haltingly proceed, is a response to needs that are characteristic of *human* infancy as understood by a Freudian: the need to regulate tension and achieve a "psychophysiological equilibrium" in the absence of an "ego" with the adaptive resources to do so for itself. Thus, symbiosis, which, for Mahler, is the apotheosis of "attachment," is a metaphor for the infant's cognitive immaturity and physical helplessness shortly after birth and consequent reliance on the mother to protect his "rudimentary ego" from disruptive stimuli. Mahler's "symbiosis," like Bowlby's "attachment," may be said to safeguard survival, but, for Mahler, the survival at stake is a distinctively *human* survival, since the symbiotic state of the first months of life consists not merely of attachment but of the "emotional rapport" intrinsic to the mother's nursing care. It is for this reason that she characterizes the beginning of the symbiotic phase as a "matrix of physiological and sociobiological dependency on the mother."[9] It is only via the maternal sustenance the infant receives *within* this symbiotic matrix that he can differentiate *from* the mother, eventually achieving his own sense of what Mahler terms "entity and identity." Compare this psychological approach with Bowlby's ethological approach, which radically dissociates attachment behavior from issues of dependence and dependency: "The fact is that to be dependent on a mother-figure and to be attached to her are very different things."[10]

Because Mahler understood the separation-individuation process to be a barometer of normal psychological growth out of symbiotic dependency, the locus of her observational research had to be a nonstructured environment in which the behavioral correlates of such growth could gain unfettered expression. This is to say that her research program presupposed an environment in which separation and individuation would be emergent properties in the natural interaction of mother and child rather than rated responses to situations created by an investigator. To inject an experimental presence into the "field" of mother-child interactions would be to compromise the status of the observations thereupon made, since such a presence, along with any experimental tasks imposed, would alter the normal psychological distance between mother and child; it would elicit the capacity for separation and individuation specific only to unnatural, if not stressful, situations.

In elaborating a research design that could capture the everyday context of growth toward separation and individuation, then, Mahler and her coworkers undertook to create and then infiltrate, unsuspectedly, a relaxed environment of mothers, infants, and toddlers at play. While available to the young mothers participating in their research projects for advice and assistance as the need arose, Mahler and her associates generally functioned as benign participant-observers, blending unobtrusively into a congenial "indoor playground" environment in which mothers could interact with their young children as they would in the home. This methodology, Mahler has recounted, reflected a conscious decision "to let the mothers and their babies show us the paths the research should follow."[11]

In *The Psychological Birth of the Human Infant* Mahler details the range of behaviors that provided observational analogues to the infant's and toddler's intrapsychic separation process. Because she wants to chart a developmental process that occurs internally over time, she must be sensitive not merely to gross acts of separation, but to qualitative aspects of mother-child interaction that are more subtly revealing of the psychological distance between the two, and hence of how the one is psychologically using the other. She must observe, that is, with the eyes of the psychoanalyst for whom manifest behavior is imbricated with clues about unconscious functioning. The following passage is especially revealing of her ability to hone in on such clues. Put differently, it bespeaks her ability to pose the right questions, that is, questions that lend themselves to observations from which inferences about an intrapsychic separation process can be made:

> How does a mother carry her child when she arrives: Like a part of herself? Like another human being? Like an animate object? How does the young infant react to the mother's taking off his wraps? Once in the room, does the mother separate herself from the child

physically and/or emotionally, or is there an "invisible bond" between baby and mother even across some physical distance? Does the mother know what is happening to her infant even though he is at some distance from her? How quickly, how readily, and how appropriately does she respond to his needs? Does the mother keep her infant in her arms a great deal? Does she make a gradual transition by taking him slowly to the playpen, for example, and staying with him until he is comfortable, perhaps offering him a toy? Or can't she wait to be rid of him, dumping him into the playpen immediately upon arrival and turning her attention to other things, perhaps her newspaper or conversation, turning to the child to overstimulate him only as her own needs demand it? In sum, we found that the observations in the infant room showed us the individual characteristics, as well as the development, of the mother in her mothering. We were able to formulate the characteristics of the interchange between mother and her babe-in-arms, of mother's interchange with her rapidly crawling or paddling older infant, with the child who begins to show interest in "other-than-mother" persons, with the vigorously exploring toddler, and with the child who begins to talk and can make his needs known in new ways. We were able to study the mother's ways of separating herself from the young infant and her responses to separation initiated by the child later on.[12]

I have alluded to the fact that Mahler's investigations into the "normal" separation-individuation process were an outgrowth of still earlier investigations that looked to the same developmental themes in an effort to explain the pathology of extremely disturbed infants and toddlers. These earlier studies, begun in the

1940s, are quite foundational to Mahler's achieve-ment.[13] They are also central to her personal history, being revelatory of the clinical preoccupations that she brought to the investigation of the normal separation-individuation process. The development of this body of work is chronicled in the memoirs; here I will pro-vide only the barest of summaries.

Mahler's early studies of infantile psychosis, culmi-nating in the publication of *On Human Symbiosis and the Vicissitudes of Individuation: Infantile Psychosis* (1968), are consonant with her later research in the assumption that the separation-individuation process is a develop-mental *achievement*. In the failure of this process to commence and hence unfold in the normal way, Mahler held, we arrive at an explanation of degrees of impairment tantamount to "childhood psychosis." This body of research eventuates in what Mahler terms the "symbiotic theory of infantile psychosis." The the-ory includes, as principal subsets, Mahler's categories of "autistic psychotic syndrome" and "symbiotic psy-chotic syndrome." The former condition bespeaks the infant's failure to *form* a nurturing "symbiotic" rela-tionship with his mother; the latter bespeaks the in-fant's failure to *grow out of* a relationship of symbiotic dependency in the interest of achieving separation-individuation. These two categories of psychotic dis-turbance signify fixations at, or regressions to, the "normal autistic phase" and the "normal symbiotic phase," which, according to Mahler, precede the separation-individuation process in all infants. Child-hood (and later adult) disturbances of "neurotic" magnitude, including character disorders, suggest that the separation-individuation process has been derailed in the course of its sequential unfolding, thereby complicating the engagement and resolution of the Oedipus complex. With such disturbances, problems dating back to the "rapprochement" subphase of the process are frequently at issue.[14] But childhood disturbances of psychotic proportions point to the fact that the process itself has not been engaged, since the infant or child has failed to emerge from, or failed to experience altogether, the necessary anlagen of such a process, to wit, a reliably satisfying "sociobiological state of symbiosis with the mother."[15] Such a child has failed, that is, to "use" the mother to make a discovery that originates *in* the symbiotic stage, but that eventually becomes "internalized" and thence leads the infant out of this stage and into the separation-individuation process: the discovery that the mother is not a "part" of himself but rather an "object," albeit a special object on whom he can depend to relieve his tension and satisfy his needs.

In the memoirs, Mahler reflects candidly on the reasons why, in the early 1960s, she in effect "switched gears," turning over to colleagues the continuing research into the forestalling of the separation-individuation process in seriously disturbed children so that she could commence studies of the "normal" separation-individuation process in healthy children. I shall not reiterate what she ably recounts for herself. I would, however, highlight one general point that the memoirs make abundantly clear: Mahler's research agenda, or, more accurately, the clinical insights that raised the questions that informed her research agenda, derive not only from her experience as a child psychiatrist and psychoanalyst but from her earlier training and research as a pediatrician—a status which, among psychoanalytic investigators of early life, she shares with the eminent British theorist D. W. Winnicott. And Mahler's pediatric concerns, the reader of her memoirs shall discover, were in turn subtended by certain facts of Mahler's own early life—facts that she not only elaborates with admirable candor but acknowledges as foundational to her clinical and developmental *Weltanschauung*.

The extent to which, and the various ways in which, Mahler's own life exemplifies her theory of development, being something of a lifelong enactment of the separation-individuation process, the reader may decide. I am content to call the reader's attention to this theme as one interesting dimension of the memoirs; they testify eloquently to Margaret Mahler's own continuing struggle for personal autonomy and professional identity, and to her successive leaps forward out of a series of personal and professional matrices, each of which possessed both nurturant and constraining aspects. In point of fact, Margaret Mahler's equivocating attitude toward the memoirs project itself during the final years of her life was in certain respects the final stage of her struggle for separation and individuation. Autobiography, in the distinctively modern form in which we understand it, presupposes a self-reflective person asking "who am I?" and "how did I become what I am?" It is for this reason that Karl Joachim

Weintraub, the historian of autobiography, believes that the genre begins with St. Augustine's *Confessions;* we search in vain in the literature of classical antiquity for the conditions of self-conscious individuality that lend themselves to modern autobiographic writing.[16] For Margaret Mahler, the writing of memoirs was especially revealing of these truths; she realized full well that candid reflections about her life and career would not only be revealing—painfully revealing—of the grounds of her individuality but would involve one further act of separation, or at least distancing, on her part. I refer, specifically, to a distancing from the Viennese psychoanalytic community that had trained her and nurtured her and a distancing from the American psychoanalytic community—or, at least, certain elements of this community—that had embraced her in 1938 and provided the supportive milieu in which she would achieve international prominence in the decades to follow. I believe that a brief review of the circumstances attending my role in the preparation of these memoirs will be revealing of these claims.

III

"A hallmark of autobiography," writes Karl Joachim Weintraub, "is that it is written from a specific retrospective point of view, the place at which the author stands in relation to his cumulative experience when he puts interpretative meaning on his past. This moment, this point of view, needs to be recaptured for a proper understanding of the autobiographic effort; so must the motivation and intention of the author for writing autobiography at all.''[17] In the case of memoirs prepared for posthumous publication by someone other than their author, questions of the author's point of view, motivation, and intention are especially salient, since the author herself cannot be said to have sole responsibility for the published version of her memoirs; allowance must be made for the role of the editor-writer who has given final shape and form to a work that would otherwise exist only *in potentia*. But the editor's role and reflections *can* be entered into the public record, providing a scenario whereby the reader can acquire perspective on the work in question. I offer the following remarks in this spirit. They will aid the reader in comprehending the self-reflective "moment" encapsulated in the memoirs of Margaret Mahler.

When, through the kind introduction of my friend and colleague Dr. Doris Nagel, I met Margaret Mahler in March 1984, I sensed at once that before me was a great but also greatly demanding woman, one with whom collaboration would likely be a challenge. She was, at eighty-seven, intellectually vital and unabashedly judgmental—in a word: feisty—and no feistier than in bemoaning her age, her frailty, and her loss of memory. I was introduced to her as an editor-writer who, having collaborated successfully with a number of her colleagues and also having pursued scholarly work in the history of psychoanalysis, could aid her in writing the memoirs she had long desired. She had laid the groundwork for this project in 1980–81, having then offered verbal reminiscences on her life and work to Doris Nagel via a series of chronologically structured interviews.[18] She herself, she averred, had neither the time nor the energy to organize the mass of interview transcripts into a narrative account of her life, though she believed that coherent memoirs could and should be fashioned out of these materials. And she very much wanted published memoirs, believing that her life and career were sufficiently interesting—and sufficiently important—to warrant a public accounting.

As an historian of psychoanalysis acutely aware of her status as one of the last living analysts with direct contact with Freud's original circle, and one whose career spanned more than six decades of work in pediatrics, child psychiatry, and psychoanalysis, I could only second her judgment and offer to help her as best I could. Dr. Mahler was, for whatever reason, well disposed toward me[19] and newly animated at the thought of actually bringing the memoir project to fruition. She packed me off with interview transcripts covering her childhood and youth, contracting me to produce a narrative account of this material for her consideration. We would see what would come of it. She was confident, I believe, that I would do what could be done, but still somewhat skeptical that the rather skeletal material at my disposal could generate memoir chapters— and perhaps equally skeptical that my skills or the skills of any editor would be equal to the task of giving her finished chapters she would find acceptable.

Ironically, it was only after Dr. Mahler had read, with satisfaction and apparently some surprise, the initial product of my efforts that I experienced, albeit gently and dilutely, the demandingness of which others had forewarned me. In a note of May 12, 1984, she announced herself "very pleased with the sample [chapter]," and in a letter of May 17, which accompanied interview transcripts covering the "Jena" and "Vienna" periods of her life, she expanded a bit: "As I told you on the phone, it was a most pleasant surprise for me that my life story lent itself to writing such an interesting chronicle through your pen. Thank you." It was in the aftermath of this expression of satisfaction that she called me several times, inquiring after my progress with kindly bluntness: "Well, what's the story with these memoirs of mine?", asking why I was taking so long in sending her subsequent chapters, and asking, furthermore, why I could not commute to New York to review passages with her at her convenience.

Following my completion of drafts of two more chapters, she, Doris Nagel, and I met in her New York apartment to discuss the work completed to date and plan for the future. At this meeting, her attitude toward the project had changed subtly but perceptibly. She professed satisfaction with drafts of chapters covering her medical education and career in pediatrics and her psychoanalytic training in Vienna, but seemed mildly diffident about the "Vienna" chapter, which recounted her brief, traumatic training analysis with Helene Deutsch and also revealed her personal relationship with her second training analyst and mentor, August Aichhorn. In preparing these preliminary drafts, I had queried her for more information about her analysis with Deutsch and also appealed to her for guidance as to the extent of the disclosures about Aichhorn she was authorizing. Clearly, she found both topics difficult to discuss. She had not, I now believe, really thought through, or come to grips with, the revelations that publication of her memoirs would entail—and this despite the fact that my coverage of these sensitive matters came directly from interviews with Doris Nagel that were to be the basis of the memoirs. When, in response to a mild demurral about the desirability of revealing her involvement with Aichhorn, I submitted that I simply did not know how to write about the "Vienna" period without discussing her relationship and subsequent affair with Aichhorn, so central was he to her professional and personal development during this time, she nodded in silent assent. She was not prepared to elaborate on these touchy issues—her anger, at the age of eighty-seven, toward Helene Deutsch, who analyzed her for a year when she [Mahler] was twenty-nine, was striking—but she was, to the end, a courageous woman, willing to concede that to have her memoirs was to own up to her loves and hates, and to offer to the public what she could recall about them.

Had our collaboration continued beyond the spring of 1984, it would have been my charge to challenge her to reflect more deeply and to recollect still more. And I believe that additional recollections would have been forthcoming, her advanced age and her stubbornness notwithstanding. For Dr. Mahler was reanimated by the preliminary drafts, which suggested that her wish to have her memoirs was, through me, realizable. Thus, in the letter of May 17, 1984, that followed her reading of the first draft of chapter 1, and that accompanied transcripts covering the "Jena" and "Vienna" periods, she spoke of:

> . . . much more to be said about the London period, which had much drama in it. Doris and I might try to reconstruct it in some more meaningful detail.
>
> A few more batches of pages will be sent to you next week containing material which was not transcribed for years, and has to be de-ciphered. Maybe I even will have to listen to the corresponding cassettes to make sense of them.

And even her letter of June 22, which marked the end of our collaboration, spoke only of a postponement of our work owing to the realization that her more active participation in the organization of preliminary materials would expedite my work. After itemizing her upcoming summer commitments, she indicated that "for the time being my priority cannot be the memoir project." She went on to say that:

> Our meetings were most helpful to me for clarifying important issues, particularly also for me to see that the material, as it now exists, is far too scattered and will need very much more preliminary work on my part to be usable without undue expenditure of time and money for the final preparation and editing of such a book.
>
> I hurry to inform you of this turn of events so that you [may] dispose of your valuable time accordingly.

Perhaps feeling that these remarks suggested her with-
drawal from the project, she added a handwritten note:
"Wishing you a good summer and hope to talk to you
sometime in the Fall." I did not hear from her again.

IV

When the executors of Margaret Mahler's estate invited me, in the spring of 1986, to complete the project I had begun with Dr. Mahler in 1984, they proceeded on the basis of a testamentary mandate that
there be a memoir of her life. This mandate testifies to
the fact that, Dr. Mahler's failure to become actively
engaged in the preparation of the narrative notwithstanding, she remained invested in the memoir project,
both emotionally and intellectually, at the time of her
death. In authorizing me to produce a narrative version
of Dr. Mahler's life, they were explicit as to my charge:
I was to produce a manuscript that derived entirely
from interview transcripts containing Dr. Mahler's
own reminiscences of her life and career. It was understood that I would not only adhere to the substance of
the interviews but would preserve, as best I could, the
tenor, tone, and language of these reflections.

For purposes of this undertaking, the executors
made available to me, along with the interviews with
Doris Nagel with which I had worked during Dr.
Mahler's lifetime, a number of additional interview
transcripts of autobiographical reflections. Of these

supplementary transcripts, by far the most important were Dr. Mahler's four interviews with Dr. Bluma Swerdloff of the Columbia University Oral History Research Office. These interviews, two of which were conducted in the fall of 1969 and two in the fall of 1974, cover much the same ground as the Nagel interviews of 1980–81. But owing perhaps to the fact that Dr. Mahler was somewhat younger at the time, they contain valuable detail that she did not, or could not, recall in the Nagel interviews. So the memoirs that follow are in fact a narrative synthesis of Dr. Mahler's Columbia Oral History interviews and the Nagel interviews of 1980–81, supplemented by the yield of a number of more topically specific interviews on her life and work conducted between 1977 and 1984. I have also had access to a number of Dr. Mahler's speeches and presentations and to several videotapes of interviews that were never transcribed. These latter documents have played a minor role in my work, providing a date here, a detail there, but generally covering in broad sweep the events and personalities recounted in far greater detail in the Columbia Oral History and the Nagel transcripts.

So what is the product of my labor to fashion a coherent narrative account, in the first person singular, of Margaret Mahler's life from interview transcripts? Although I can provide no assurance that Dr. Mahler would have approved of every presentational particular in the manuscript, down to sentence structure and word choice, I am confident that she would have readily embraced the manuscript as *her* memoirs in substance, style, and tone. I make this claim in full recognition of the fact that, as a writer and historian, I have brought my own sensibilities to bear, however subliminally, on the preparation of this work. Had another historian-writer, with his sensibilities and values, undertaken the same task, he would necessarily have produced a manuscript that differed from mine in subtle matters, viz., in the continuous lexical and organizational choices that are intrinsic to the structuring of any narrative. But if, in approaching the task, he had, like me, made his agenda Margaret Mahler's agenda, he could not have arrived at a finished product that differed substantively from this one in the eventful particulars recounted, the personal judgments accompanying them, and the language in which both are cast.

I do not, then, contest the commonplace that historians "select" the data out of which they fashion their narratives. But I do submit that, in the preparation of this manuscript, whatever selective biases I have brought to the task operate at the compositional periphery rather than the narrative core of the work, since I have drawn on a compact set of complementary interview transcripts to produce as full an account of Margaret Mahler's life as possible, squeezing as much detail as possible out of *all* the transcripts rather than playing them off one against the other, or otherwise shaping one narrative out of disjunctive or contradictory sets of reflections that could have yielded alternative accounts.

In fact, in all the interviews, Dr. Mahler was remarkably consistent in her recollections and interpretations of events, her characterizations of people, and her reflections about her life and career. The interviews differed only in concentrating on different aspects of her life, and hence in providing different pockets of detail to be incorporated into a larger synthesis. In submitting that my particular synthesis is one she would have happily embraced, I have the judgment not only of her executors and the numerous colleagues who read the memoirs as they were being prepared but, more tellingly, Margaret Mahler's own plain satisfaction with the draft chapters she reviewed prior to her death. I have gone beyond the transcripts only with respect to minutiae, checking and, where necessary, amending names and dates in the interest of the factual accuracy that was so important to Dr. Mahler. Otherwise, I have been the editorial instrument through which Margaret Mahler tells her own fascinating story.

1 • Sopron

Sopron, where I was born on May 10, 1897, was a small border district, or *comitat,* in Western Hungary, closer to Vienna—a mere forty miles away—than to Budapest. The true status of the town as a bridge between the political and cultural life of two nations is embodied in the fact that it also had an Austrian name, Ödenburg, and, via a plebiscite held in 1921, residents could opt for either Hungarian or Austrian citizenship. This borderland (if not "borderline"!) existence impressed me early in life with the political and linguistic polarities that define our lives, and left me straddling the fence between two traditions. My childhood attempt to mediate between these two traditions was tantamount to a personal version of the Imperial Compromise, or *Ausgleich,* which from 1867 had linked the Germans of Austria and the Magyars of Hungary within a tenuous "Dual Monarchy."

Consider the issue of language. My father, Gusztav Schönberger, who was born in Ferto-Szent Nikos, another town near Sopron, accepted Hungarian as his mother tongue. On the other hand, the parents of my mother, Eugenia Wiener Schönberger, came from Lakenbach, a German-speaking Schwabish town. Although my mother was educated in a Hungarian school, she spoke only German with her parents and subsequently failed really to master Hungarian. Years later, in my psychoanalysis, I realized that my younger sister, Suzanne, and I had spoken Hungarian with my father but, when my mother entered the room, automatically switched to German. These linguistic circumstances understandably contributed to my divided political allegiance. To this day, I feel a strong tie to Austrian culture, deriving from my early proximity to Vienna; at the same time, I recall my early feeling for Hungarian nationalism in opposition to Habsburg imperialism.

The district of Sopron, with its fine examples of Baroque architecture, was the birthplace of Liszt. Within the county, one finds the town of Eszterhaza, where Haydn served as *Kapellmeister* for many years. At the turn of the century, Sopron had achieved a modest renown that belied its status as an inconspicuous little border district. As a repository of "high" Hungarian culture, it regularly commanded side visits from the many notables who journeyed to Vienna.

Within Sopron, we lived in the so-called *Gyoery Palota* (Palais of the Railroad Company), a complex of apartment houses inhabited by the executives of the famous railroad that went through the town. This self-contained community, which included tennis courts and little gardens, provided an active social life, especially for the young. The homey atmosphere of this time and place has vanished, perhaps surviving only in the novels of the Hungarian writer Jokai.

My father, a graduate of the medical school of Vienna University, was a general practitioner who held the rank of chief public health officer of the district. He had an office in the beautiful town hall but conducted most of his business out of our house. Socially prominent in the community, he held membership in the exclusive local "club," being one of only two or three Jews so honored. My mother did not share my father's active social life. Her world was the world of the household, where she prided herself on being an excellent cook and homemaker. Despite the fact that my father adored her, she was, throughout my childhood, a deeply unhappy woman.

In the nature of things, I became very much my father's daughter. I came far too early—nine months and six days after the wedding—and was very much unwanted by my mother, who was a mere girl of nineteen at the time. Very beautiful, very narcissistic, and greatly pampered, she blamed my father for my untimely arrival, holding him accountable for the loss of her "nuptial handkerchief." In her anger, she had as little to do with me as she could. During my first year of life, when I was quite sickly and had sleep disturbances, it was my father who, with my nurse, arose at night to attend me. My symbiotic stage of life was difficult: I must have been full of frustrated rage at the rejecting mother whom I greatly loved nonetheless.

The arrival of my sister, Suzanne, four years after my birth only aggravated my sense of maternal rejection. She was very much a "wanted" child, and she awakened our mother's maternal instincts—instincts that, for me, had lain dormant. For my sister, my mother got up at night; she accepted and loved the younger child in a way she never accepted and loved me. I believe it was my observations of my mother's loving interaction with my sister—and the way it contrasted with her interaction with me—that guided me into pediatrics and psychoanalysis and, more specifically, into my subsequent investigation of the mother-infant dual unity. I do not think it an exaggeration to say that my own mother and sister represented the first mother-child pair that I investigated. Even in early childhood, I was regarded as a very watchful child, whose intense gaze drew frequent notice. I have been told that, during my first year, when I would not sleep at night, my father would instruct my nurse to put me down, and she would reply: "How can I put her down? She stares like a lynx." This visual overvigilance may initially have been a response engendered by the uncaring mother who, so I thought, wanted me dead.

If I learned anything from observing my mother's loving ministrations to my sister, it was how *not* to treat one's older child. My mother's continual demonstrations of affection and solicitousness in my presence only fueled my sense of victimization: I was angry at my mother and full of contempt for the sister who, as I saw it, had it all too easy. I recall an incident from early childhood in which my anger gained expression. My sister, then a toddler of perhaps two, put her cheek to a hot iron. When my mother came home, she became hysterical, dancing around the room with the child as she sobbed uncontrollably. My own reaction to this sad spectacle was one of glee and contempt. My sister was such a dumbbell, I thought, to put her cheek to a hot iron.

It was out of my lack of confident expectation, of basic trust in my mother's feeling for me, that I turned to my father. I have been told that at four and a half, I watched my mother cuddling my baby sister and saying to her: "I have brought you into this world, I suckle you, I love you, I adore you, I live only for you, and you are my whole life." To which I replied: "And I, I was born by my father" (*Und mich hat mein Papa geboren*). I cannot remember this incident, but I do recall, as a poignant screen memory, a somewhat later incident. My mother, who had developed a breast abscess from nursing my sister, told me to my face that she had not nursed *me,* only my sister. And when the physician, who was my father's boss and predecessor, came to the apartment to tend my mother's wound, I remember very well my childhood rage, which took the form of the thought: "serves you right to have had such a little creature chewing up your breast."

My mother's uncaring rejection alienated me irretrievably from the household that was her domain. She was the slave of our big apartment, which she maintained as a veritable shrine. Trespassers were not permitted. Even my father was forced to take his afternoon naps in his office at the city hall. On those rare occasions when I brought friends home, they were ungraciously received. My friends were intruders, just as my father's patients were intruders. For my mother, everything revolved around the appearance of the household, not the needs and wants of its members.

As I look back to this early period of my life, I see my mother's preoccupation with the apartment as the manifestation of a severe neurosis which rendered her insensitive to the feelings of others. I still recall my eighth birthday party—the first and last of my childhood—as a moving example of my mother's lack of consideration. The high point of the party was to be a tombola, a lottery, and my mother summarily decided that the grand prize would be my cherished chocolate collection of beautiful animal figures in which I took great pride. She bribed me: in order to have the birthday party, I had to consent to give away my prized collection. Although my mother at least agreed to divide the prize between two children, she ultimately gave the entire collection to a little girl who was a distant relative on her mother's side. This only added to my desperate unhappiness at parting with my cherished possession. As the party ended, I cried inconsolably. There would be no more birthday parties.

It was to my father's world, the world of the intellect, of science, of medicine, that I turned in early childhood. In contrast to my mother, who would not even let me enter her inner sanctum, the kitchen, my father treated me as if I were his son. I recall how he boasted to his friends: "I have a daughter with whom I can discuss mathematics and politics."

In fact, it was my father's eager adoption of me as his "son," and my willing acceptance of this role, that confounded my childhood gender identity.* It never occurred to me, and my mother never gave me reason to believe, that I could be accepted as a pretty young girl. My father was of no help in this respect, his buttressing of my intellectual self-esteem being very much at the expense of my feminine self-esteem. I recall an

---

*Nor did the peculiarities of the Hungarian language help. The Hungarian term *fiam,* with which my father addressed me, has the dual meaning of son and daughter.

incident from early childhood, after my sister and I had been photographed by the local court photographer. My mother made a derogatory remark about my photograph to the effect that I looked homely or ugly. To which my father immediately replied: "But the photographer said that her beauty cannot be appreciated by ordinary people." This incident stands out in my mind because it was, in my recollection, the only positive remark my father ever made about my appearance. From the time of this incident until I reached my sixties, I barely looked at myself in the mirror. I absolutely denied the fact that I was, or had ever been, an attractive woman.

Further incidents come to mind that testify to my difficulty in embracing a feminine identity. When I was a schoolgirl, my father would greet my periodic avowals of love for various male teachers with the following pat reply: "You are man enough for yourself" (*Du bist dir Mann's genug*). When my sister, at thirteen, was already beginning to attract swarms of young men, I, at seventeen, was busily reading everything available on Einsteinian relativity! On those occasions when I did socialize, I aroused a reaction in my male companions that was very different from that of my sister. I recall how I intimidated one of my dancing partners during a promenade at the annual dinner dance of the Lehne Institute, a famous boarding school in Sopron. The annual dance was a socially important event in town, and only the female offspring of Sopron's high society were invited to attend. During the promenade in question, my partner and I got to talking about

God. When he asked me where God would be, I replied, "In the fourth dimension." The boy had no idea what I was talking about, the idea of a "fourth dimension" being beyond his comprehension. Suffice it to say that my reply made him quite uncomfortable and that we never went promenading again.

Existing well outside the narcissistic orbit of my mother and sister—my mother "collected" my sister's beaux and, herself a beautiful woman, came alive when my sister entered adolescence—I tended to deny my own femininity entirely. I refused to believe that any man worth having could love me; if one per chance expressed any feeling for me, he was instantly devalued.* Never having learned how to compete with other women as a woman, I learned instead how to avoid defeat as a woman in a world of men. In short, I developed a strong drive for independence at an early age—an orientation with which my father was in full sympathy.

Yet my father, in his failure to appreciate that I was not his son, merely compounded my problems. I grew up torn by a contradiction of which I was only partly aware. On the one hand, in identification with my father, I tried very hard to be "man enough" for myself. On the other hand, I envied my sister her feminine conquests, even as I wanted my father to treat *me* like

---

*I would characterize this belief as the main "complex" that I brought to my training analyses at the time I began psychoanalytic training. My analysis with Willi Hoffer, in particular, aided me greatly in coming to grips with the issues that sustained this belief.

a pretty little girl in need of chivalrous defense. But my father's paternal solicitousness seemed reserved for my sister. When I married, at the age of thirty-nine, he was less than enthralled by the event, even though he liked my fiancé, Paul Mahler. When poor Paul came to Sopron formally to ask for my hand, my father said to him: "You must know what you are doing; she is not average (*Durchschnitt*)." Psychoanalytically speaking, my father meant: "Watch out, for whatever her strengths and weaknesses, she is not castrated, and you had better watch out not to get castrated by her." My future husband, to his infinite credit, did not take flight at this point but stayed and went through with the wedding. My father arrived late to the dinner that followed the marriage ceremony. Although a generous man, he asked me to reimburse him for the expense of the wedding dinner even before it was over. One might say that he resented my marriage!

My educational decisions followed from my identification with my father and my corresponding resolve to escape my mother and the household. After completing the six-year program of the local "Higher School for Daughters" (*Höhere Töchterschule*), I had the choice of attending either a *pensionat* (i.e., a finishing school) in Switzerland or preparing for a career by attending a gymnasium (i.e., a high school) outside of Sopron. Sopron itself, be it noted, had a fine educational system that included a gymnasium, but girls were not permitted to attend it. Nor, for that matter, could they attend the grammar or middle schools that fed into it. And so it was that my aspirations for a gymnasium education were directed to Budapest. While either a Swiss *pensionat* or a Budapest gymnasium would have gotten me away from my mother, I opted for the gymnasium, partly to test my father: I could not quite believe that he would allow me to undertake a rigorous course of academic study that was assuredly not for provincial Hungarian "daughters," and that could pave the way for a career in medicine.

In fact, I had by this time formed the fantasy that my father would be greatly upset if his "little girl" decided to become a physician. This fantasy, which undoubtedly derived from my own intrapsychic conflicts, blossomed in the context of my surreptitious reading, during late childhood and early adolescence, of the medical books in my father's library. At some point along the way, it occurred to me that medicine, which dealt with the body, including the diseased body and the "dirty" sexual body, was itself taboo. My father, so I convinced myself, would never give me his blessing to pursue a career that would bring me into daily contact with the body.

But my fantasy was just that—a fantasy—and my father took my announcement to pursue academic studies at a Budapest gymnasium in stride. It rather suited him, after all, that I should have the career of a boy. Whether or not I was his "son," I certainly had the brains and personality to study in the manner of a son. And so, in 1913, I became the second woman from Sopron to leave the hometown to pursue the higher education normally reserved for men. Of course, even my father's support did not overcome my continuing conflicts about academic pursuits in general and a medical career in particular. After successfully completing the gymnasium, for example, I did not apply straight away to medical school, dabbling instead in the more acceptable "female" field of art history for a semester. I seemed intent on making it as difficult for myself as possible to pursue my "male" career goal. I not only procrastinated endlessly, submitting my medical school application at the very last minute, but continued to crave a more conventional female role even as I moved ahead with my "male" pursuits.

But I am moving ahead of my story. My move to Budapest at the age of sixteen was a turning point in my life, even though the circumstances of the move seemed inauspicious enough at the time. I was to stay with my mother's favorite sister, Irma Wiener Herezeg, who had made it clear that she did not particularly like me. Like my mother, she preferred my sister. Years later, I discovered among my sister's effects her correspondence with this aunt: they had spoken very fondly of one another but not very well at all about me! Tante Irma, to whom I later extended financial assistance, survived the end of World War II; the Nazis probably let her go on living because of her advanced age. She had two children, a daughter who was schizophrenic and died before the Nazis occupied Budapest, and a son who had been a good friend of mine and was killed by the Nazis.

It was during my two years at the Vaci Utcai Gimnazium in Budapest that I encountered psychoanalysis under the auspices of the Kovacs household. Shortly after beginning my studies, I became the "best friend" of Alice Szekely-Kovacs (later Mrs. Michael Balint), a gymnasium classmate. Her mother, Vilma Kovacs, was a grande dame of Budapest society who later became a distinguished Hungarian training analyst. She had been one of Sandor Ferenczi's early analysands and, at the time of my entry into the household, which was some time after the termination of her analysis, she counted Ferenczi as a good friend. I was fortunate to have her as a supportive "mother away from home" during my gymnasium years in Budapest. Her husband, Fritz Kovacs, was one of the best-known architects in Hungary, having designed many prominent public buildings.

The Kovacs's beautiful villa on Nap Hegy (Sun Hill) was a kind of salon, a psychoanalytic household in which I was warmly received, a veritable adopted daughter free to come and go at will. An object of affection, I was given the pet name of "Sonjicska," associated with Sonja Kovalevsky.[1] The Kovacs's frequent dinner parties included Ferenczi, Michael Balint, Geza Roheim, and the painter Robert Bereney[2] among the guests. At one such party I was introduced to Ferenczi, who appeared to like me.

It was in the context of these intellectually stimulating gatherings, and especially of my introduction to Ferenczi, that I was first drawn to psychoanalysis. So, for that matter, were Alice Szekely-Kovacs and Emmy Balint (Michael's sister). The three of us, all gymnasium classmates, got hold of Ferenczi's German transcription of Freud's Clark University lectures of 1909, which we read clandestinely, under the school bench, so to speak. The Clark lectures were an ideal point of entry to this new science, providing a clear, accessible picture of how psychoanalysis "works" and what one can do with it. Shortly thereafter, I obtained a copy of Freud's *Three Essays on the Theory of Sexuality,* which I read avidly and with very mixed emotions, vaguely sensing that the work embodied a great discovery. From this early acquaintance with Freud, I emerged with a strong appreciation of the idea of the unconscious—a heady notion indeed for a sixteen-year-old school girl from provincial Hungary!

But it was my direct contact with the people who gathered at the Kovacs's home that had the deepest impact on me. One lived psychoanalysis on Nap Hegy; the air we breathed was tinged with Freud's pioneering discoveries. I remember Ferenczi asking me about my father and my telling him how I saw to it that he had his afternoon nap undisturbed by the flies. Ferenczi just listened; if he was formulating an interpretation, he never shared it with me. In fact, Ferenczi was quite fond of me, later encouraging me to apply to the Vienna Psychoanalytic Institute for training. I have already remarked that our hostess, Vilma Kovacs, after undergoing an analysis with Ferenczi, became an analyst herself. She later wrote a psychoanalytic paper about the scrotum, "The Bag of Fortunatus," which, although barely known today, still strikes me as a classic. Michael Balint, who, at the time, was also a gymnasium student, was also drawn to Ferenczi and would later become his executor and heir. He was then as interested in mathematics and anthropology as in psychoanalysis, and his interest in Alice, whom he would later marry, was an additional reason for his frequent presence in the Kovacs household.

Psychoanalysis, for me, begins in Budapest, and especially in the drawing room of the Kovacs's villa where Vilma Kovacs entertained her distinguished circle of friends. It was the knowledge of my accepted "insider" status in this Budapest circle that was a constant source of comfort during the eventful period of my analytic training in Vienna, where I was very much an "outsider." Throughout this later period, I made frequent visits to Budapest, always being revivified by the warmth and acceptance of the Budapest circle. Eventually, I became a sort of "visiting professor" to the Budapest Psychoanalytic Society, instructing society members on the application of Rorschach testing methods to clinical work. It was during the time of these frequent visits, as well, that I became a close friend of Alice's sister, Olga Szekely-Kovacs. Under her married name of Olga Dormandi, she would become a very well known artist, especially acclaimed as a portraitist after moving to New York in the early 1940s.

The lasting influence of the Budapest circle on my life and career ranges beyond the support and acceptance it provided during the difficult years of my analytic training. No less important was the role of this circle in shaping both my developmental outlook and my clinical concerns. The influential Hungarian analysts with whom I mingled at the Kovacs's villa—Ferenczi, Herman, Bak, Benedek—made a very special contribution to analysis that, to date, remains insufficiently appreciated. The whole idea of the mother-infant dual unity, for example, originates in their theoretical and clinical perspectives. This developmental viewpoint did not gain expression in the German or Viennese psycho-analytic literature of the time. It is not even found in the later work of Anna Freud. At her Hampstead Clinic, the mother-child pairing was surely recognized, but the child was evaluated separately. "Leave the mother in the waiting room; she is tired," the Hampstead analysts would say. Anna Freud and her collaborators were concerned almost exclusively with the intrapsychic, which they believed to be the only proper domain of psychoanalysis. Indeed, the intra-psychic *is* the main thing, but as I have undertaken to show over a lifetime of research and writing, the intra-psychic only evolves out of the differentiation from the initially undifferentiated matrix of mother and child. To speak this way in psychoanalytic circles as recently as twenty or thirty years ago, to invoke the "environ-mental" preconditions of intrapsychic development, was to be branded a heretic; and it is still this way at certain psychoanalytic institutes. It was even worse at the Hampstead Clinic during the 1930s and forties, be-cause the clinic analysts had to take great pains to differ-entiate their position from that of both Melanie Klein and D. W. Winnicott. It was Winnicott, it will be re-called, who claimed that there is no such thing as a baby without a mother.

Of Ferenczi, I should perhaps say a bit more. I had strong feelings for him that I never had for Freud, per-haps because he was, for me, so much more accessible than Freud. Following our acquaintance in the Kovacs household during my gymnasium years, our paths crossed in 1920, around the time he was just beginning to experiment with the "active technique" that would subsequently earn him Freud's disapproval. At the time, rumors were already being heard that Freud was treating Ferenczi badly, ignoring his new ideas; Ferenczi himself was known to complain that Freud had not touched his (Ferenczi's) negative transference when he (Freud) had analyzed him.

Although I was hardly in a position to adjudicate the technical controversies spurred by Ferenczi's work, I was and am convinced that he was a brilliant man, one of the most imaginative of Freud's early followers. I believe that the assumptions that underlay his technical innovations were not only sound but have proven essential to the evolution of analysis in the decades following Freud's death. It was Ferenczi, first and foremost, who appreciated how deeply certain analysands have to regress in the analytic situation if analysis is to have its curative effect. Unlike Freud, he was not afraid of deeply regressed patients; in this respect, he was well ahead of his time. Ferenczi's maternal ministrations to these severely regressed patients—he may even have bottle fed some of them—embodied his recognition of the fact that certain early deprivations must be addressed and overcome before the work of analysis can proceed; he anticipated much of the recent work on the psychoanalytic handling of developmental arrests. Freud, by contrast, always professed an utter antipathy toward psychotics. I recall the letter he sent to István

Hollós, Ferenczi's coworker, after Hollós sent him a manuscript, *Beyond the Yellow Walls,* for an appraisal. Freud confessed that he always felt ashamed or uneasy when he confronted human beings who were no longer human beings. He thereupon declined an appraisal of Hollós's work, claiming he could not render an objective judgment because his attitude toward psychotics made him unable to occupy himself with the contents of the book.[3]

In 1916, I left the Kovacs's nurturant household. It had provided an oasis during the two years of gymnasium study when I was unhappily living with my aunt. As gymnasium work drew to a close, the students who had been welcome members of this curious psychoanalytic salon went their separate ways. Alice Kovacs went to the University of Berlin to study anthropology, and I simultaneously agonized about, and planned for, a medical career.

2 · *Medical Training Between the Wars*

My matriculation in the University of Budapest in September 1916 brought an abrupt and painful separation from the Kovacs circle that had sustained me during my two years of gymnasium study. I continued to live with my mother's sister for a short while but, still feeling somewhat unwelcome in her home, shortly moved to the university where, for the next two years, I shared a furnished apartment with several classmates. My decision to begin medical training followed a period of vacillation when, in line with the eclectic interests of my friends in the group, I considered alternative careers in the sciences and humanities. The Kovacs circle, it will be recalled, was a psychoanalytic study group only in the broadest sense; our interest in Freud and his discoveries was but one of a mosaic of cultural preoccupations that traversed mathematics, biology, anthropology, sociology, and education. At various times, I considered following my friend Alice Kovacs in the study of anthropology, Robert Bereney in the study of art, and my own natural talent for mathematics.

In fact, my entrance into the medical school was, as I mentioned, preceded by a semester of study in aesthetics and art history. Although I was very much interested in the arts, and especially in sculpting, I lacked the talent to pursue an artistic carer. To make matters worse, the Budapest faculty in these fields was not particularly distinguished, and I was frankly bored to death by my semester of courses. And so it was that I resolved to put aside what was essentially a hobby and to pursue the profession to which I had long aspired.

Having made this decision, I presented myself to the dean of admissions of the medical school, gained admission, and, as of January 1917, the beginning of the second semester of my first year of university study, became a medical student. But I was far from relieved at this point: I began to brood at once about how I would "confess" this development to my father. I used the Easter recess as the occasion to journey back to Sopron to break the news to him. And, lo and behold, my persisting fantasies of his disapproval notwithstanding, he took the news with total equanimity, simply remarking, "Darling, if that makes you happy, I am entirely with you."

In finally deciding to pursue psychoanalysis via the study of medicine, I picked a course that diverged from that of most of my friends, our common interest in Freud notwithstanding. I have by now written enough to suggest that my father exercised a strong and perhaps critical influence in this decision. When, during my childhood, he became aware of my strong attraction to his work, he overcame whatever anxiety was attendant to the realization that medical training was a truly pioneering ambition for a young girl in Hungary. I recall peripatetic conversations with him during adolescence when, having secretly accepted that fact that I would become a physician, he cautioned me to avoid certain bleak medical specialties. Rather than medicine or surgery, he preferred that I choose a "dainty" specialty more suitable for a woman, ophthalmology, for example. I recall a number of discussions in which we discussed the pros and cons of various specialties and during which he undertook to enlighten me as to the "shady side" of medicine. His concern lest I enter an unsuitable specialty was really the only basis for my fantasy that medicine was taboo and that my father was opposed to my becoming a physician per se.

I recall, in particular, my father's low estimation of psychiatry. Predictably, he shared the contemporary view of psychiatry as a hospital or academic specialty concerned primarily with the institutional care of psychotics with exceedingly poor prognoses. On numerous occasions, I observed him escorting agitated psychotics to the state hospital in neighboring Pressburg (Bratislava), there being no such hospital in Sopron. As chief public health officer of the district, he was obliged to see that acutely disturbed individuals (e.g., individuals experiencing catatonic outbursts) were rendered harmless. This world of psychiatry was obviously far removed from the world of psychoanalysis I encountered in the Kovacs household. But my father could hardly be expected to apprehend the difference between psychiatry, as he knew it, and psychoanalysis. To his credit, he followed my evolving professional interests in an open-minded way: when he learned that I had become interested in psychoanalysis, he read Freud.

My transition to the life of a medical student was trying. After three semesters of preclinical studies at the University of Budapest, several classmates and I jointly decided to transfer to the medical school at the University of Munich to begin our clinical training. Our little entourage, be it noted, included one young man who was not a medical student. I refer to J, an ardent suitor with whom I had had an on again, off again affair during my two years of preclinical training. When, following completion of the second semester of the 1918–19 school year, my classmates and I decided to leave Budapest, J desperately wanted to marry me. Since I was not at all ready for marriage, he resolved to accompany me in my educationally inspired relocation.

In fact, there were a host of reasons for the move to Germany. The repressive, Communistic Horthy regime, which gained power in Hungary in 1920, immediately instituted the system of *numerus clausus* (closed number) that drastically reduced the number of Jews permitted to pursue a university education. Although my departure from Budapest preceded the Horthy regime by a year, the handwriting was, by 1919, clearly on the wall. As a Jew who was also a woman, my chances of being allowed to complete my training in Budapest were quite small. And even if I had been permitted to complete my training, the political circumstances of life under the Horthy regime, which included the agitation of opponents to the regime, were hardly conducive to quiet study. Moreover, I had by then resolved to specialize in pediatrics, and the outstanding teachers and researchers in the field were all in Germany at the time. Pediatrics, I should perhaps explain, represented a compromise of sorts: it would enable me to be what my father was, while simultaneously accommodating my desire—perhaps my outstanding "feminine" trait—to work with children. At the time, the desire to become a baby doctor, and thereupon to be a practicing physician like my father, coexisted with the equally strong desire to become a psychoanalyst like Ferenczi, the warm father figure I had encountered in the Kovacs household.

A familial circumstance capped the reasons for my departure from Budapest. My younger sister, who played the harpsichord, wanted to pursue her music studies with a certain teacher at the Odeon Conservatory in Munich. Since she was neither old enough nor responsible enough to live there on her own, my parents would only let her pursue her career in Germany under my wing. I resolved to transfer to the University of Munich in time for the fall semester of 1919.

My life in Munich was very adolescent, very confused, and very intense. Academically, I quickly became a star student, highly regarded by classmates and teachers alike. Yet, my acute sense of insecurity belied the persona of a successful medical student. This insecurity was aggravated by the gender confusion that was the legacy of my childhood and that came to the fore when, to my amazement, I became the object of attention of a number of eligible young men. I was still very much a provincial girl from Sopron who, lacking self-confidence, found it hard to believe she could be a desirable sex object for any suitable, level-headed young man.

My main personal conflict at the time continued to center around J, who was adamant in his courtship. I devalued him, unwarrantedly, and despite being attracted to him, did my best to discourage his advances. Ours was a back-and-forth relationship, not at all happy, that lasted until the young man left for a stint

Margaret Mahler's mother, Eugenia Wiener Schönberger, beautiful, pampered, and demanding, rejected Margaret, who was born nine months and six days after her marriage. With her younger daughter Suzanne, born four years after Margaret, Eugenia's maternal instincts blossomed, aggravating her older daughter's unhappiness. *(From the Estate of Margaret S. Mahler.)*

Mahler's father, Dr. Gusztav Schönberger, was a pillar of Sopron society. He loved Margaret as a son, valuing her scientific aptitude while denying and even disparaging her femininity. *(From the Estate of Margaret S. Mahler.)*

From top, clockwise: Margaret Mahler at five years old; her sister Suzanne in early adolescence; Margaret at eight with Suzanne at four. Throughout childhood, Margaret resented Suzanne, whose prettiness and femininity were appreciated by both parents and who elicited maternal affection that Margaret was always denied. *(From the Estate of Margaret S. Mahler.)*

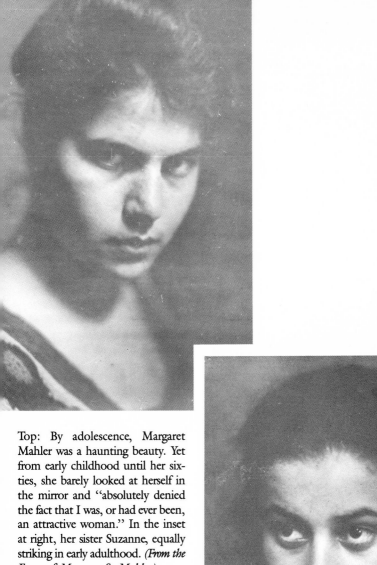

Top: By adolescence, Margaret Mahler was a haunting beauty. Yet from early childhood until her sixties, she barely looked at herself in the mirror and "absolutely denied the fact that I was, or had ever been, an attractive woman." In the inset at right, her sister Suzanne, equally striking in early adulthood. *(From the Estate of Margaret S. Mahler.)*

Mahler, as a Budapest gymnasium student in 1917–18, shown here (sixth from left) on an outing with classmates and her Greek teacher. *(From the Estate of Margaret S. Mahler.)*

As a medical student, Mahler received most of her clinical training at the University of Jena. Here (bottom row, sixth from left), adorned in a wreath, she joins friends in celebrating the traditional "midsummer festival" (*Sondwendfeier*), ca. 1920. *(From the Estate of Margaret S. Mahler.)*

Mahler, at age nineteen, in a Hungarian identification/passport photo, 1916. *(Margaret S. Mahler Papers. Manuscripts and Archives, Yale University Library.)*

From 1923 through 1926, Mahler received graduate training in pediatrics in Vienna at the clinic of Clemens von Pirquet. She is shown here with one of her young patients. *(From the Estate of Margaret S. Mahler.)*

Mahler recalls herself as one of the first Viennese physicians to buy a car and make house calls. *(From the Estate of Margaret S. Mahler.)*

Top: August Aichhorn, here in a photo ca. 1925, was Mahler's most important mentor. Both a psychoanalyst and the leader of Austria's child guidance movement, he drew Mahler into his fold shortly after her arrival in Vienna in 1922, giving her free access to his network of municipally sponsored child guidance clinics. He became Mahler's training analyst in 1927, following Helene Deutsch's termination of Mahler's first training analysis. *(From the Estate of Margaret S. Mahler)* Right: Mahler in the mid-1920s, around the time she began her psychoanalytic training. *(From the Estate of Margaret S. Mahler.)*

Margaret Mahler and Paul Mahler in the 1930s. They met in Vienna while she was completing her analytic training and married in 1936. He was a chemist and co-owner of a Viennese cordial factory begun by his father and uncle. He was also, as Margaret recounts, "a very cultured and gentle man." *(Photo of Paul Mahler from the Estate of Margaret S. Mahler. Photo of Margaret Mahler from Margaret S. Mahler Papers. Manuscripts and Archives, Yale University Library.)*

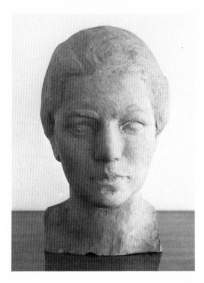

Top: A bust of Margaret Mahler by the Hungarian sculptor and Mahler's great friend, Beni Ferenczy. Ferenczy completed the bust in 1938, on the very night before Austrian chancellor Kurt Schuschnigg left Vienna for Berchtesgaden, where he capitulated to Hitler's demands. *(Copyright © 1985 Andrew Holbrooke.)* Bottom: It was Ferenczy who wrote Mahler in 1945, telling her "in a wonderfully touching letter" of her mother's death in Auschwitz. He is shown here in Budapest in 1961. *(From the Estate of Margaret S. Mahler.)*

of army service. I was relieved, but my anguish about the relationship testified to the psychological baggage that accompanied me to Munich. Specifically, I was still dominated by my father's disapproval of any and all inclinations toward involvement with the opposite sex. Unlike other upper-middle-class European Jewish families, my parents had never undertaken initiatives to acquaint me with eligible young men in town—the only sanctioned way for a young woman to make the contacts that could lead to courtship and marriage. As a result, I had never established a secure sense of myself as an attractive woman. To the contrary, I had unconsciously internalized my parents', and especially my father's, strange resistance to the notion that I should ever find fulfillment as a woman. In so doing, I had effectively embraced the meaning of my father's devaluation of my feminine strivings: that I was a neuter. But how to act the "role" of a neuter when I was pursued by eligible young men to whom I felt attracted—this was at the heart of my personal difficulties in Munich.

These difficulties, as I have observed, coexisted with great success in my studies. Even as a young foreign student, I was appointed a *Co-Assistentin* by Professor Pfaundler, the eminent chairman of the Pediatrics Department, and henceforth became very involved with the Pfaundler Clinic attached to the department. I was likewise honored with the status of *Co-Assistentin* by Dr. Rudolph von Degkwitz, another prominent pediatrician, assisting him with experiments aimed at developing a serum to prevent measles according to a method recently devised by the Italian pediatrician Caronia. At the time, measles was a very dangerous disease when contracted in adolescence or early adulthood. Caronia believed that if a child exposed to measles was given intravenous injections of the whole blood of an adult, he would either not contract measles at all or contract only a very mild case. Von Degkwitz and I tested Caronia's hypothesis by injecting children exposed to measles with a few cc's of whole blood from an adult relative's compatible blood. I became so familiar with the technique that much later, after graduation from medical school, I was asked by colleagues to immunize, or render "morbilli resistant," their children. Alternatively, if their children had already been exposed to this, at the time, rather grave childhood disease, I was asked to ameliorate the gravity of the case of measles that would inevitably ensue.

More important than the questionable medical success of this procedure was the personal impact of my work with von Degkwitz: I was so thrilled by the experimental research that our work entailed as to be convinced that my future lay in this direction. As a student and, later, as a full-fledged *Hilfärztin,* or "apprentice physician," I was intent on conducting research that went well beyond the limits of my narrowly defined "assisting" role. I engendered a great deal of opposition in the process. Several years after the work with von Degkwitz, for example, when I was training in pediatrics in Vienna, I was engaged to do extensive experiments with starting sedimentation rates by the Swedish researcher—or one of his close associates—who developed the method and described the significance of sedimentation rate studies.[1] My academic superiors tried to prevent my participation in this research, simply because I then had the lowly status of a student "co-assistant." I persisted undaunted, experimenting with sedimentation rates in the homes of children, and taking on my rounds certain university-based nurses who offered to assist me. But I encountered opposition every step of the way, and the results of my research were never prepared for publication.

But to return to Munich: my academic success and budding research interests could not insulate me from the anti-Semitic fog that was fast enveloping Germany, including the German academic establishment. The Kapp Putsch of 1920, prelude to the demise of the Weimar Republic, occurred during my medical studies in Munich. I did not then understand the context of the Putsch, nor was I sufficiently interested in contemporary politics to grasp its implications. But it was quite evident that, following the Putsch, hostility toward Jews became increasingly overt. Local residents did not yet have the legal means to rid themselves of Bavarian Jews, so they turned with a vengeance on Jews who had come to Germany from other countries, and especially from countries to the east.

My Hungarian classmates and I were ripe targets for local abuse: we had dared to gain admittance to a Bavarian university, we treated German patients, and we even presumed to live in Munich. Nor was my sister Suzanne, a music student, exempt from public hostility. The city administration did what it could to make life difficult for us. It passed an ordinance prohibiting "aliens" from dwelling in Munich proper, forcing us to take up residence in the suburb of Solln bei München. Not content with this sanction, it seemed intent on souring life in the suburbs. One day, as my sister and I were having lunch at the boarding house or "pension" where we stayed, we were suddenly picked up by the police and, without any reason, thrown in jail. A lawyer friend of the family managed to secure our release several hours later, but we were given no explanation (much less an apology) for what had transpired. Apparently, the sole point of the "arrest" was to intimidate us in the hope of inducing us to leave even "suburban" Munich. The local officialdom was less than subtle in making us feel unwelcome!

As I suffered mounting indignities, I came to feel doubly victimized, not only by the authorities who resented my presence, but by my younger sister who, lacking any instinct for danger, continued to insist that we stay in Munich. In her own delicately manipulative way, Suzanne managed to dominate me with her needs, knowing full well that our parents would not permit her to stay in Munich if I departed. Our increasingly distressing predicament notwithstanding, she preferred to continue her harpsichord studies in Munich even though, during the Putsch, shooting had broken out all around the Odeon Conservatory.

Economic conditions did not make Munich any more bearable. The inflation rate was absolutely unbelievable. If one wanted to buy a pair of shoes, one had to queue up to such a long line that by the time one reached the store, one no longer had enough money to pay for the shoes. The whole situation, compounded by continuing difficulties with J—who stayed in touch even after beginning army duty—finally enabled me to overcome my sister's controlling influence. By then, I knew exactly where I wanted to go and what I wanted to do: I wanted to go to the University of Jena to study with Ibrahim, the Professor of Pediatrics and author of the important chapter on "Pediatric Neurology" in Emil Feer's *Pediatric Textbook,* the major work in its field.[2] My sister, despite herself, was obliged to return to Vienna while my several classmates from Budapest also transferred elsewhere.

Jena had much to commend it at the time of my arrival in the spring of 1920. The city was then in the forefront of the German trade union movement, and its glassworks and Schott factory received national attention for their avant-garde sponsorship of adult education, especially for the factory workers. These factories, together with the university, offered a rich cultural life revolving around evening schools (which attracted the most eminent lecturers of the day), beautiful concerts, and periodic festivals. Jena's proximity to Weimar, with the latter's own remarkable cultural and intellectual life, was part and parcel of its attractiveness. The academic success that characterized my two-year stay in Munich followed me to Jena as well. Ibrahim immediately accepted me as a co-assistant in the private clinic where he treated ruminating and pylorospastic infants—no mean feat for a medical student, since Ibrahim was the leading pediatric neurologist of Germany. But I had always been the favorite of my professors, and Ibrahim's appointment enabled me to learn a great deal about two baffling infant illnesses.

In the early 1920s, treatment methods for these two conditions were still experimental. Ruminating infants voluntarily regurgitate food which has already reached the stomach, remasticate it, and swallow it a second time; their gastrointestinal distress generally points to an underlying emotional disturbance. At the time of my work with Ibrahim, one accepted treatment approach was to position the maxilla (i.e., the upper jaw bone) of the ruminating infant so that he could neither ruminate nor really enjoy his food, only bring it up. With respect to infants suffering spasms of the pylorus (i.e., the circular opening of the stomach into the duodenum), there were several treatment options. One could attempt corrective surgery or feed the children heavier food, which, so Ibrahim believed, would better remain in the stomach.

Despite the physical immediacy of these disorders, they achieve real significance as dramatic psychosomatic illnesses of early infancy. The emotional factors that entered into these conditions were so overwhelmingly apparent that even physicians with entirely somatic orientations could not deny their importance. Ibrahim himself, though having no contact with psychoanalysis, must have been particularly interested in these factors; otherwise, he would have had little reason to maintain a private clinic for patients with these conditions. The emotional dimension of these two psychosomatic conditions of early infancy had such an impact on me that the medical issues involved in treating the infants soon receded in importance.

As I reflect on my early exposure to these troubled infants, I recall an episode at Ibrahim's clinic which, more than any other medical or surgical occurrence, has remained indelibly impressed in my mind over the decades. It concerns an atrophied little boy of three or four who was brought to the clinic one day by his father, a woodcutter from the countryside. The child appeared to have nothing wrong with him beyond his very low weight and general failure to thrive. He was the woodcutter's only child, and the two had never been separated prior to the clinic stay. I do not know how the father was persuaded to leave the child at the clinic; he had what I would later term a "symbiotic" relationship with his little son.

Ibrahim, understandably interested in this perplexing problem, accepted the child as an inpatient. He died that very night. The father returned the following day, intent on taking his son back to the forest with him. He told us of a dream he had had the preceding night in which he felled a tree in the forest and the tree was his son. Following the dream, he resolved to reclaim his son, only to find him dead on arriving at the clinic. I was baffled and overwhelmed by this poignant sequence of events. I could not medically explain what had transpired, but I had the feeling that something very strange and mysterious and yet very understandable in an existential way had taken place. The father and his small son had obviously been very, very close. I do not know whether the mother was alive, but, quite clearly, the father was both mother and father to the child at the time of his death. What I had experienced, in pristine form, was an atrophic child who, free of any ascertainable medical problem, could not survive once his symbiotic bond with his father had been ruptured. I do not recall how Ibrahim and his staff undertook to explain the death of the child. But I do recall that we all shared a feeling of awe, an unspoken conviction that medical science could not give us an adequate answer to what had transpired.

There were happier times in Ibrahim's clinic to balance this tragic incident. I learned from him how important play is for children and how curative love can be. Ibrahim was an unorthodox pediatrician in his day and age, willing to play with his young patients in an effort to understand them and learn from them. I recall weekends when he would lock the door to the nursery, his *privatstation*, get down on his hands and knees, and literally play "horsey" with the children—a rather undignified position for the chairman of the department, but one revealing of his great affection for his small patients. Ibrahim was a strange man. Like most of the other prominent pediatricians under whom I trained (Schick, Wagner, Noble, von Pirquet), he was fully absorbed in his relationship with children, yet lacked a family life of his own. A rough tabulation suggests that seven of the nine pediatricians with whom I had contact as a student and assistant physician were either unmarried or married very late in life.

Unfortunately, my professional growth under Ibrahim and continued success with medical studies were balanced by personal difficulties similar to those I had experienced in Munich. The anti-Semitism which had, in part, induced me to leave Munich was by now rampant throughout Germany. Although Jena's workers were among the most educationally advanced and politically progressive in Germany, Jena's academic world was extremely reactionary. Although the university professors were generally liberal, the student body, supported by a handful of reactionary teachers, was a hotbed of pro-Nazi sentiment, even as Weimar, symbol of German democracy, was only a few miles away. As things turned out, I appealed to the latter to overcome the persecution of the former.

As a Jew from Hungary, I had been admitted to medical school at Jena over the protests of the student body organization, the Jena chapter of the German-wide *Allgemeiner Studenten Ausschuss* (General Student Board). During my first year at Jena, this local chapter of the national student organization convened a meeting in an attempt to annul my admittance to the student body. As I listened from the courtyard of the university, I heard the president of the chapter ostracize me without mentioning my name; he gave a speech lambasting the "East European Jewess" who had been accepted into their Aryan institution. I recall going home with two good friends, who asked me to whom the speaker had been referring; I had to tell them it was I.

In point of fact, I was in real danger of being expelled from the university despite the fact that I continued to distinguish myself academically and clinically. I resolved to do something about it. I travelled to Weimar where I had several influential friends, including Professor Peterfy, an anatomist of Hungarian descent. Peterfy, after listening to me, was moved to protest my abusive treatment to university officials. Not content with this gesture, I went to Karlsruhe to speak with the physician Edwin Blos (father of the distinguished American analyst Peter Blos), who, I was told, had considerable influence with the Jena student organization.[3] As it turned out, Blos's intervention with the General Student Board was decisive: I remained in Jena and eventually graduated from the university.

Before graduating, however, I journeyed to the University of Heidelberg in the spring of 1921 for my final semester of study. As the political situation in Germany worsened—especially for Jews—Heidelberg seemed to be an oasis, a "fun city" with excellent medical facilities as well. I completed my Jena degree at Heidelberg partly to escape the hostile atmosphere of the university, but also to escape J who, having earlier followed me from Budapest to Munich, had more recently seen fit to follow me from Munich to Jena, where he continued to make my life miserable. He attempted to coerce me into continuing our relationship and, in that connection, endlessly reproached me for refusing to promise I would not date other men. We had one unpleasant showdown after another.

It was in Heidelberg that I finally managed to shake this dogged but, by now, unwanted admirer. In anticipation of my move to Heidelberg, J had written my father, warning him to keep an eye on me insofar as I had dropped him (J) and was about to go down the primrose path. Obviously, the young man did not know to whom he was writing. My father, in characteristic fashion, expressed his complete confidence in me and advised J to desist in his ill-fated and unwanted pursuit. To be sure, my father had ulterior motives as well: he was quite happy that his daughter was in no danger of marrying this "son of a tailor from Szeged." I saw the last of J in Jena.

Heidelberg was a welcome respite from the turbulence, both academic and personal, of Jena. As my semester of study there was acceptable to the Jena medical faculty, it did not delay my graduation. Although the medical curriculum in Heidelberg was very stimulating, I was not as fully preoccupied with my studies during this last semester as I had been in Jena. I do recall some brief contact with the eminent pediatrician Moro (of the "Moro reflex").

But mainly my intellectual life in Heidelberg blossomed outside the university. I became friendly with a fascinating group of people gathered around the philosopher Karl Jaspers. Among these new friends were the poet Friedrich Gundolf; the sociologists Emil Lederer and Nicholas Halasi; and, most important, Karl Mannheim and his wife Julia. Max Weber, the sociologist, was also a member of the circle, but I had no direct contact with him. Following my introduction to these eminent academicians by my fellow Hungarian, Julia Mannheim, they doted on me as their "nice little girl." I don't know that I contributed much to their heady discussions, but it was flattering nonetheless to

be welcomed into the households of the Lederers and
Mannheims and befriended by so distinguished a coterie of thinkers. The experience was, of course, reminis-
cent of my happy acceptance in the Kovacs household
in Budapest; the home of the Lederers, in particular,
was for me another Nap Hegy.

I was particularly impressed by Jaspers. I listened in-
tently to his lectures and the animated debates that followed them. I read everything that figured in the
groups' discussions, including Jaspers's work on psychopathology. Psychoanalysis was not yet in the air in
Heidelberg, although, in later years, the Mannheims
became close to analysis. Karl was highly regarded as a
scientist by Ernst Kris; Julia undertook psychoanalytic
training after the Holocaust with no less a mentor than
Anna Freud and eventually became an analyst.

These happy days in Heidelberg were clouded only
by serious physical illness. At the age of fourteen or
fifteen, I had experienced abdominal pain with symptoms pointing to a "strangulation" of the intestines.
Although I now believe that my symptoms had psychological meaning and that my entire condition was a
species of psychosomatic intestinal problem, the treatment I then received was an appendectomy. The operation was apparently not very successful because I
thereafter experienced intermittent attacks of severe abdominal pain. Although these attacks generally sub-
sided with anti-spasmodic medication, they intensified
in Heidelberg to the point that I became quite ill. I
recall experiencing severe attacks in the presence of the
Jaspers circle, during which these towering intellects

would desist from their heady discourse and do what they could to help me. I have a particularly poignant memory of Karl Mannheim simply sitting beside me and observing me with great sympathy during one such episode. The academics gathered around Jaspers were frankly fearful that I would die. It was at this juncture that I consulted Enderlen, a leading Heidelberg surgeon. In consultation with my internist, he diagnosed serious obstructions making a partial Hirschsprung's disease (a congenital disorder of the colon rectum, which is unable to relax to permit passage of stool). Frustrated with the severe pain and longing to be well, I acceded to the surgeon's recommendation that I undergo what was at the time a drastic operation: resection of part of the colon, i.e., a partial colectomy.

Before attempting this then dangerous procedure on a person still considered a minor—antibiotics were not yet available—the surgeon needed my father's consent. On being apprised of my condition and the proposed course of action, my father refused to give his permission for the colon operation and resolved to come to Heidelberg at once. As it turned out, however, he managed repeatedly to postpone the trip to the point that the surgeon had to operate before his arrival, permission or not. I say that my father "managed" to postpone the trip because I believe that, deep down, he *wanted* to come late because he simply could not bear the prospect of my undergoing a partial colectomy, with the great risk this procedure then entailed. Fortunately, after all the drama attendant to my condition, the surgeons found nothing but some severe adhesions that could be removed without disturbing the integrity of the colon. And so there was an end to my problem.

After completing my semester in Heidelberg over the summer of 1921, I returned to Jena to take the written and oral examinations required for graduation. I did beautifully, being one of only two students to graduate magna cum laude at the beginning of 1922. But, perhaps predictably, several unnerving experiences clouded this happy finale to my medical training. The anti-Semitism that had followed me from university to university throughout the course of my medical training came back to haunt me on the eve of my graduation. An anti-Semitic faculty member, Professor Abel, learned that I had completed a course of instruction in laboratory technique—so anxious was I lest I fail to realize my medical ambitions and have nothing to fall back on!—at the same time as I had been pursuing my medical studies. He remonstrated that I should not be allowed to graduate, since I could not have attended to my medical studies adequately while devoting time to these laboratory studies. His objection was of course belied by my record—both academic and clinical—to which Ibrahim and several other supporters forcefully called attention. My record and my faculty supporters prevailed, and I was instructed to proceed with my final examinations.

Several untoward incidents compounded this trying rite of graduation. The oral examination in ophthalmology, for example, was scheduled for a morning following a night when the entire group of examinees had been assigned clinic work until three o'clock. On the day of the examination, we all went to our oral exam and complained to the professor that we were in no condition to sit for the examination. I recall being rather confused, sleepy, and outspoken in my indignation. After a few minutes, the professor relented, stating: "Ladies and gentlemen, I think you should come back tomorrow. Do you want to know when? When little Schönberger has had enough sleep." So we returned the next day and took the examination.

I behaved no better with the pediatrics examination. Being something of a prima donna, expected by professors and classmates alike to perform with distinction, I grew fearful at the last moment that I could not live up to their (and my own) expectations—I failed to report for the exam. This self-indulgent action could have delayed my graduation by several months. Fortunately, it did not. Professor Ibrahim came to my rescue, sending his adjunct to my apartment to assure me that, however well I performed, it would be good enough. He urged me simply to come and get the examination over with. But I still felt unable to comply. It was a full ten days later that Ibrahim conducted a special examination for me. I passed with flying colors. My dissertation—the concluding exercise that was the sequel to satisfactory completion of the final examinations—was in the area of pediatric hematology: "Thrombocytopenic Purpura in Childhood."

My academic trials and tribulations did not come to an end with my graduation in Jena. My diploma did not entitle me to practice medicine in Germany; I needed a medical license and, not being a citizen of Germany, could not qualify for one. This fact of medical life, along with the economic hardships deriving from the continuing inflation, induced me to leave Germany. I sought to go "home" to Vienna, a mere hour away from Sopron. In Vienna I could continue my pediatric training at the famous clinic of Clemens von Pirquet and eventually undergo psychoanalytic training, thereupon regaining contact with the preoccupations that had directed me to medical school in the first place. Obtaining medical licensure in Vienna would present no problem, since by then I had become an Austrian citizen.*

On arriving in Vienna near the end of 1922, I spent several months preparing for the qualifying examination in forensic medicine which German-trained physicians had to pass in order to obtain an Austrian license.** It was termed a "nostrification" examination, that is, an examination which validated a medical diploma obtained outside the country. I recall studying with Mrs. Bernfeld, second wife of the analyst Siegfried Bernfeld, who was preparing for the same test.

I passed the examination in 1923 and was rewarded with a new medical diploma and a license to practice

---

*As I noted at the beginning of chapter 1, residents of Sopron (Ödenburg) could opt for either Hungarian or Austrian citizenship via plebiscite; I opted for Austrian citizenship because I wanted to train and eventually practice in Vienna.

**Vice-versa, Austrian-trained physicians who sought a German medical license had to pass an additional examination in skin and venereal diseases.

medicine in Austria. An interesting story surrounds my taking of the test. At this time, which is to say near the end of 1923, Vienna newspapers were devoting much space to a famous criminal case involving a Mrs. Vukobrankovich, a very clever child murderer. It so happened that my nostrification examination in forensic medicine was administered by Professor Albin Haberda, who, quite coincidentally, was the court-appointed lawyer for the accused Mrs. Vukobrankovitch. After I handed in my examination paper, Professor Haberda quickly scanned it and then addressed my twenty or so younger male colleagues who were still busily at work since, unlike me, they were taking not only the examination in forensic medicine, but the whole gamut of medical qualifying examinations. "You see, gentlemen," he announced, "the Frau Dr. Schönberger and Mrs. Vukobrankovitch have given me much cleverer answers than you!" The next day, when I presented myself at the pediatric clinic of the great Viennese pediatrician, von Pirquet, everyone knew the story of how I had been compared, albeit in a complimentary way, with the murderess Vukobrankovitch.

3 · *From Pediatrics to Child Psychiatry*

My early months in Vienna were inauspicious enough. Prior to leaving Germany, I had made all the arrangements to apprentice myself to von Pirquet's clinic, the most prestigious university-affiliated children's clinic in Austria.[1] But these arrangements notwithstanding, my transition was far from easy. Simply finding suitable living quarters was a project in itself. I recall being teased by Bélà Schick, von Pirquet's codirector, about my frantic hunt for a furnished room in Vienna—no easy feat on my limited budget. Of course, this "limited budget" was self-imposed. I might have asked my father for the money to rent a more adequate apartment. But I could not: my "father complex," largely unanalyzed at the time, prevented me from appealing to him for financial assistance. And so it was that, for the first month or so, I was an irregular attender at the clinic and invariably arrived complaining about the bedbugs in my miserable room!

With von Pirquet himself, I had considerable contact. A great antifeminist, he liked me almost despite himself and singled me out to assist him with his ongoing statistical and epidemiological studies, sparing me, on such occasions, the onerous chore of working in the pediatric *ambulatorium,* or outpatient clinic. It was at von Pirquet's behest, for example, that I went to all the kindergartens and grade schools in Vienna, measuring the tonsils of several thousand Viennese school children. From these data, von Pirquet and I established that the hypertrophy or enlargement of the tonsils has two peaks, the *hypertrophia tonsillarum infantilis* of early life and the *hypertrophia tonsillarum puerilis* of the tenth or eleventh year.[2] Ironically, it was on account of von Pirquet's continuing use of me as a research and statistical assistant—I was always being asked to report to the "chief," as he was called—that I learned less clinical pediatrics than would otherwise have been the case.

But von Pirquet's appreciation of my research skills did little to mitigate his absolute horror at the prospect of having any woman in a position of authority. Thus, when I later requested a promotion from "apprentice" (*Hilfärztin*) to "assistant" pediatrician, he replied, "I will never have a woman as an assistant. You are very smart, and I like you very much, but if one is a woman, and especially if one looks like you, one should marry and have children." The remark about the desirability of a woman who "looked like me" marrying instead of pursuing a profession was repeated on more than one occasion. I recall, as well, von Pirquet's comment the first day I donned glasses at the clinic. Inspecting me carefully, he remarked, "Do me a favor. Put those glasses in your pocket," by which he conveyed the clear meaning that he couldn't stand them on my face! This disparaging estimation notwithstanding, I idealized von Pirquet and regressed to the point of being well-nigh "in love" with him.

I also became strangely attached to one of von Pirquet's senior assistants, Edmund Nobel, with whom I coauthored three research papers in 1924–25. Nobel was a capable if unimaginative pediatrician, far less gifted than von Pirquet's other associate, Béla Schick. But he was unsurpassed in his devotion to von Pirquet and spent much of his time monitoring the activities of the "chief." He must have had a premonition that von Pirquet was entertaining suicidal thoughts—a premonition borne out several years later, in 1928, when von Pirquet and his wife committed suicide together. Although Nobel did not attract me as a man, in the course of our collaborative work I came to expect that he would propose to me. I invited his solicitousness, probably in the unconscious expectation that marriage to him would make me a full-fledged member of von Pirquet's "family." It was in this pragmatic, career-oriented context that I entertained what I would describe as "reverse Pygmalion fantasies" toward Nobel. At our frequent platonic rendezvous in the coffee houses of Vienna, I fantasized transforming this unemotional and difficult man into a romantic suitor—one who would love me not as an "adult" woman, but as a capable and attractive young pupil. It was a desexualized intellectual fantasy that I lived out for years.

Despite my high regard for von Pirquet and his associates, I was secretly appalled by the detached, sterile way in which they undertook to treat very sick children. I recall, in particular, my horror at the then popular "nem system" of feeding infants, that von Pirquet created and employed. Via this sytem, each hospitalized infant was placed in a sterilized cubicle of which part of the walls consisted of glass panels. In order to preserve the bacteria-free environment, the infant was bottle-fed via a nipple inserted into the cubicle. Feedings consisted of a portion of milk carefully measured in "nems," i.e., units of nutrition corresponding to the caloric value of one gram of breast milk.[3] There was no physical contact with the infants whatsoever during this feeding procedure.

My personal sensibilities about infant care were better served by the rival pediatric institute where I spent my summers, Leopold Moll's Institute for Mother and Child Care (*Reichsanstalt für Mutter und Säuglings Fürsorge*).* Moll was in the vanguard of pediatric researchers who appreciated the vital role of mothering in the treatment of sick babies. His institute thus espoused the credo, then progressive to the point of being avantgarde, that a baby not only "belonged" to its mother but that the presence of the mother (or mothering person) was essential if a sick baby was to get well. At the Moll Institute, then, infants and young children were admitted for treatment *with* their mothers. Moreover, in order to implement even more effectively his treatment philosophy, Moll established under the aegis of the institute a school for pediatric nurses. As part of the nursing school program, each student nurse was assigned one of the sick babies admitted to the institute, so that each baby had the benefit of additional "maternal" care in the person of a "private" nurse who also happened to be a loving student nurse.

---

*From 1923 through 1926, my summer work at the Moll Institute included accompanying children's transports on Institute-sponsored trips where young children at risk for tuberculosis were taken abroad for five or six weeks to a kind of spa. For each of these four summers, I accompanied the children across the Adriatic to Italy. After delivering them to the spa, I used my payment to fund private explorations of Italy, especially Venice, Florence, Ravenna, and Siena.

Many of these babies came to the Moll Institute
with the severe alimentary disturbances rampant at the
time. These disturbances, then grouped under the
heading of "pedatrophy," were characterized by severe "toxic" diarrhea and associated vomiting. Such
infants, who presented in a malnourished, desiccated,
and frequently marasmic state, died in droves at von
Pirquet's clinic; it never occurred to either von Pirquet
or any of his senior associates that such infants might
survive if their mothers were available to attend them.
At the Moll Institute, on the other hand, each such
infant had the benefit of maternal care in the persons
of both his mother and one of the compassionate and
dedicated student nurses. I have especially vivid memories of the latter, donning masks and carrying their
little patients around day and night, "loving" them
out of the worst doldrums. And, miraculously, these
children, who were every bit as sick as those treated by
von Pirquet and would likely have died anywhere else,
frequently responded to this solicitous care. Via the
loving ministrations of their assigned student nurses,
they emerged out of their comatose, toxic states, their
diarrhea stopped, and in most cases, they slowly became well.

Of course, the statistics of the day did not bother to
look beyond the realm of the somatic, that is, the
body, in assessing issues of morbidity and recovery. I
mentioned my experience at the Moll Institute to von
Pirquet and his associates, but such psychological considerations were far removed from their real interests,
and they did not take the input of students seriously

in any event. I have always reproached myself for not having the courage of my convictions and pursuing the matter then and there. Specifically, I should have written a scientific paper systematically comparing my observations at von Pirquet's clinic with my observations at Moll's institute.

What could I have said in such a study? For von Pirquet, the child was merely a diseased organism for which optimal treatment was treatment in an antiseptic environment. For Moll, on the other hand, the child, however organically impaired, was a whole human being; and, given the child's humanity, treatment consisting of nourishment and medication was not only insufficient, but positively poisonous if devoid of the human ingredient of loving care. My experience at the two clinics bore out the infinite superiority of the latter approach over the former. In many ways, Margaret Ribble's revolutionary, if now virtually forgotten, book *The Rights of Infants: Early Psychological Needs and Their Satisfaction* (1943) makes the case that I could have made, and should have made, on the basis of my firsthand observations in von Pirquet's clinic and Moll's institute. She argues, persuasively, that the emotional feeding of the infant is every bit as important as the actual physical feeding. It was only when I emigrated to America with my husband in 1938 and renewed a friendship with Ribble that began at the time we both studied at the Vienna Psychoanalytic Institute, that I realized how profoundly right she had been in this classic work.

My work at von Pirquet's clinic and Moll's institute

was supplemented by the flourishing pediatric practice that I ran from my tiny apartment in the Albertgasse. I opened the practice some two-and-a-half years after arriving in Vienna. It marked my acceptance of the fact that von Pirquet would never promote me to the more prestigious role of clinic "assistant" and that, for the time being, I would have to earn my living as a practicing pediatrician. My "office," which was also my living quarters, was nothing but a large dining room (replete with dining room furniture that my landlady would not put into storage) and, attached to it, a small anteroom. To my amazement, a number of very wealthy Viennese brought their children to my curious apartment. Although I have only dim memories of specific cases, I recall being constantly worried about my sick children; many required hospitalization, and I saw them in the hospital as well. When I began adding analytic cases to my pediatric work load several years later, it was in these same unlikely circumstances. I recall feeling great relief when my burgeoning work in child analysis permitted me to taper off my pediatric management of very ill children.

My transition from the world of pediatrics to that of child psychiatry and psychoanalysis began shortly after I arrived in Vienna in 1922, thus anticipating by some four years my formal training as a candidate of the Vienna Psychoanalytic Institute. Shortly after becoming established at von Pirquet's clinic, I was approached by Willi Hoffer. Hoffer had just founded an innovative journal in the area of remedial education, the *Journal for Psychoanalytic Pedagogy* (*Zeitschrift für psychoanalytische*

Pädagogik), and he invited me to contribute to it. It was through Hoffer that I was drawn into the child guidance movement and introduced to its pioneering exponent, August Aichhorn. In the early 1920s, Aichhorn organized and ran for the Vienna city administration a network of child guidance clinics, eventually becoming chairman of the child guidance clinic of the Vienna Psychoanalytic Institute in 1932.[4] He was in addition close to the Budapest circle (Alice Szekely-Kovacs, Michael Balint, Geza Roheim, Sandor Ferenczi) of which I had earlier been a part. And so Aichhorn was favorably disposed toward me and, following my introduction by Hoffer, immediately accepted me into his fold. Since, in addition to my clinic appointments, the city of Vienna had appointed me a "youth and welfare physician" (i.e., a school doctor), I gained immediate access to Aichhorn's network of guidance clinics. He invited me to accompany him on his roving clinic "rounds" whenever my schedule permitted.*

Aichhorn was a mysterious man who led a strange and charmed life. A character at once striking and elusive, he prided himself on his contacts with the criminal underworld of Vienna and, often enough, seemed able to turn these contacts to good use. I recall discussions with him in which, in a quasi-serious vein, he spoke of attending "gang" meetings in which youths plotted their illegal activities. He spoke the delinquent's language, so to speak, and could make these

---

*Peter Blos and Erik Erikson were other frequent attenders of Aichhorn's clinic rounds in the Viennese public schools.

children feel so comfortable that they would share with
him their secrets without any fear of betrayal. On the
basis of his unusual "fieldwork," and through the cul-
tivation of innumerable sources who trusted him,
Aichhorn achieved extraordinary insight into the delinquent's mind and an extraordinary knowledge of crime
and delinquency in general. He prided himself on being able to predict certain happenings in the world of
the demimonde. Though these happenings were generally minor crimes or delinquencies, I recall how, on
one occasion, he predicted a major jewel theft two
weeks before it occurred.

While these reflections are not a proper occasion for
a lengthy exposition of Aichhorn's therapeutic technique, I should perhaps comment briefly on the dis-
tinctive use of psychoanalysis that informed his counseling activities with delinquents. One gets a taste of his
therapeutic style from his major work, *Wayward Youth*
(1925), but mere reading of the book does not adequately convey how his remarkable understanding of
the dynamics of delinquent behavior translated into his
theory of treatment.

First of all, it should be noted that the "delinquents" of whom I speak were not outright criminals
in the contemporary sense; Aichhorn recognized them
as the abused or misunderstood children that they
were. His counseling work with these children fell into
two stages. In the first stage, he made himself available
to the delinquent child as a love object and an ego
ideal. In other words, he cultivated and then used an
intensely positive transference to facilitate the "way-

ward youth's" identification with him. When, via this positive transference relationship, the child became dependent on him, Aichhorn used the leverage imparted by this dependency relationship to "show" the child that that he (the child) had chosen his delinquent life-style on the basis of past frustrations, abuse, or misunderstandings, but that this life-style was not appropriate to current circumstances. He was a master at drawing the unconscious motivation out of a child's recital of circumstance and happenstance and then confronting the child with the underlying reason for his delinquency. But his counseling did not end with the simple imputation of unconscious motive or his transference-fueled persuasion of the child to abandon a delinquent life-style. Rather, these counseling strategies ushered in the second stage of treatment in which Aichhorn undertook to make the child, in his own words, "as neurotic as he can be made" in order to render him analyzable.

Throughout the entire process, Aichhorn consistently gave the young person the benefit of the doubt; he had a remarkable intuitive gift for making the child believe that he was always on the child's side. He was able to retain the complete trust of the child regardless of what confessions he elicited—and he elicited confessions without any difficulty whatsoever. I believe that Aichhorn's greatest therapeutic legacy for me was this ability to inspire the complete trust of young patients, to make children feel utterly at home in the therapeutic dialogue. It is well-nigh impossible to define this subtle skill in terms of therapeutic technique, and I believe I imbibed it from him via a type of osmosis. This capacity for a special rapport, a completely reassuring empathy with young patients, stood me in good stead throughout my career. It enabled me, in the early 1940s, to interview disturbed children at the New York State Psychiatric Institute before large audiences—to the shock and dismay of certain colleagues who did not understand that, via our special rapport, the child being interviewed was oblivious to the existence of anyone but me, the presence of an auditorium of observers notwithstanding.

Without elaborating further, let me simply state that my time with Aichhorn during his consulting work at the various child guidance clinics was pivotal in my career. He was the most powerful influence of my formative years, and my perspective on children and their problems owes more to him than to anyone else.

My contact with Aichhorn complemented my exposure to child psychiatry, such as it was, under the auspices of the von Pirquet clinic. It was, to put matters plainly, exceedingly meager and, to the future analyst, exceedingly reprehensible. Within the clinic, there was a kind of subclinic or department of remedial education (*Heilpädagogik*), which, in its range of services, fell somewhere between what we would now term a child guidance center and a child psychiatry service. Professor Erwin Lazar, the chief of this department, espoused a very questionable and potentially traumatizing attitude toward children with psychiatric problems. The children brought to the service were predominantly boys who evinced either learning difficulties or any of a host of psychological problems then subsumed under the rubric of "conduct disorders." Lazar insisted on immediately examining the genitals of all these children. And if, as was frequently the case, he discovered that a boy had a testicle that was not fully descended, he scheduled the child for surgical repair at once. Self-evidently, these children left the clinic different than they entered it, emotionally speaking. But such was the state of "child psychiatry" at the time: the genitals were implicated in virtually all maladaptive or delinquent behaviors, and a then widely accepted surgical "cure" for genital abnormality was the prescribed treatment. I was horrified by what I observed in this department; it was utterly antithetical to everything I then believed, and to everything I would come to believe more strongly still, following my psychoanalytic training.[5]

Since Lazar's department of remedial education represented "child psychiatry" as it existed at the time, members of the Vienna Psychoanalytic Institute were invited to attend, and occasionally to make presentations before the clinic. By way of reciprocity, members of the department were invited to attend Anna Freud's lectures and certain meetings of the institute. It was on one such occasion that I was approached by Helene Deutsch. Noticing me at the meeting, she was reminded of her promise to Ferenczi to interview me with an eye toward taking me into analysis. I had, with Ferenczi's help, made application to the Vienna Psychoanalytic Institute on arriving in Vienna and had been interviewed at the time by Paul Federn and Grete

Bibring. Following our chance encounter at the institute meeting, Mrs. Deutsch, too, granted me an interview. Following the interview, she advised me that she was putting me on her "waiting list" for a training analysis. It was only in 1926, some four years after I had arrived in Vienna, that she informed me we could begin our analytic work.

4 · *Becoming a Psychoanalyst in Vienna*

I had come to Vienna to become a psychoanalyst. Although pediatrics consumed most of my time and energy for the four years following my move, analysis—and the prospect of analytic training—remained a steady preoccupation. My commitment to an analytic career was solidified by my contact with Aichhorn and Hoffer while I was still a pediatrician. Equally important, my enthusiasm for Freud and analysis was rekindled during my periodic visits to Budapest from 1922 to 1926. I looked forward to my stimulating conversations with my friends Alice and Michael Balint and, somewhat more periodically, with Ferenczi. At each of our reunions, my friends managed to convey their clear expectation that I should receive analytic training and eventually become an analyst. Prior to 1926, I had directly approached Paul Federn and expressed my desire to have a training analysis. As Federn never followed up on my request, I was content to rely on Ferenczi to expedite this formal point of entry into the Viennese psychoanalytic world.

And it was Ferenczi who approached Helene Deutsch on my behalf. When Mrs. Deutsch informed me in the spring of 1926 that I could begin my training analysis with her the following fall, my excitement was tempered by the insecurity that had followed me throughout my academic career. In particular, I was nervous about my heretofore fragmentary reading of the psychoanalytic literature, a concern that was aggravated by the Vienna Psychoanalytic Institute's policy that candidates should refrain from reading the literature while their training analyses were underway. Characteristically, I resolved to read and absorb as much analytic literature as I could during the summer of 1926. During my vacation in Budapest, I alternated assiduous reading with pleasant boating excursions on the Danube with Alice and Michael Balint. I took advantage of these outings to "grill" my two friends about everything I should know before beginning my analysis. They were bemused by my frantic questioning and urged me to forget about the subject matter of analysis, just to relax and let the training analysis "happen."

As things turned out, my first formal experience with Viennese analysis proved far from satisfying. At my preliminary interview with Mrs. Deutsch, she had impressed me as a kind of empress—not regal, perhaps, but an empress nonetheless. She was a striking woman, and my initial attitude was one of admiration and awe. I spun quite a fable around her beautiful eyes. I knew she came from Poland and, in an adolescent way, I equated her with the Madonna of Chenstockow, a very beautiful Polish madonna. In fact, my expectations toward her were of an altogether adolescent sort. I had always been treated as a gifted and precocious favorite child—by my father, by Vilma Kovacs, by the Mannheims, and, to a degree, by Ferenczi. In short, I arrived in Vienna convinced of my own specialness and, at my initial interview, I fantasized that I would also have a "favorite child" relationship with my analyst, Mrs. Deutsch.

I was to be gravely disappointed in this respect. Not only was I deprived of the status of a favorite child, but Mrs. Deutsch seemed intent on making me feel like a second-class citizen within the ranks of analysis. In our very first analytic hour, she was explicit as to the circumstances of my treatment. She had taken me into analysis, she remarked, 90 percent because Ferenczi had asked her to do so, and only 10 percent because I seemed to be "a nice human being" (*weil Sie ein liebes Mensch zu sein scheinen*). And from this point on, my chief preoccupation in the analysis was to prove to her that she had the actual formula reversed: that I was in reality 90 percent "a nice human being" whose career had been only marginally helped along (10 percent) by Ferenczi. In the course of the first session, Mrs. Deutsch proceeded to tell me, summarily, that I had a "sticky libido" (*klebrige libido*). As if to avenge myself for this disparaging remark, I had a dream the following night: I sat on a newly painted toilet seat and became stuck.

Mrs. Deutsch saw me in analysis for some fifty to sixty sessions. Her apparent ambivalence about the analysis was reflected in her frequent last-minute cancellations of my appointments. Her chambermaid would call me at my office at least once a week, advising me that Mrs. Deutsch could not see me that day owning to this, that, or the other matter. As it turned out, I averaged no more than three or four sessions a week, and the analysis was further punctuated by all manner of vacations, including quite lengthy breaks for Christmas and Easter. After some thirteen or fourteen months elapsed, Mrs. Deutsch finally informed me that she was terminating my training analysis because I was "unanalyzable." She never gave me a direct explanation for this judgment, but I already suspected the reason she had been ambivalent about my analysis in the first place, and I subsequently learned how she had cast her dislike for me.

The "reason" to which I refer concerned the matter of my analytic fee. Given my modest circumstances, I did not feel able to pay the customary fee for the training analysis. Now I could certainly have appealed to my father to help me on this score. He was not a wealthy man—his fixed salary was alredy strained by the high costs of my sister's continuing musical studies— but he could probably have secured a loan on my behalf. The fact of the matter, however, is that I did not want my father to borrow money so that I could pay for my analysis like anyone else. I came to Mrs. Deutsch convinced that I was, and ought to be, an "exception." Moreover, in the years preceding my training analysis, I had been reassured by my friends that the Vienna Psychoanalytic Institue had a policy of accepting "deserving" candidates who received their training analyses at minimal cost. And if there was a policy of providing for such deserving candidates, then surely I must be one of them. I "deserved" only the best, as Ferenczi himself had told me. It was on these terms then—as a deserving candidate who would be forgiven the usual analytic fee—that I began my work with Mrs. Deutsch. And it may well have been the financial arrangement attendant to my analysis, and the implicit claim of entitlement that it entailed, that sabotaged the analysis from the outset. As my friend Jenny Waelder-Hall later told me, anyone who knew Helene

Deutsch would have known that she could not analyze without payment.

Fanny von Hann-Kende, a friend and well-known pathologist from Budapest, had come to Vienna to be analyzed by Mrs. Deutsch around the same time my training analysis began. Although Fanny's analysis would eventually become a training analysis, marital difficulties—she was then getting a divorce—prompted her to seek treatment when she did, and family circumstances made it urgent for her to get through the analysis as quickly as possible and return to Budapest. Fanny's analysis with Mrs. Deutsch thus took place concurrently with mine, and it was a source of considerable bitterness to me that Mrs. Deutsch was able to see my dear friend five or even six times a week during the same period when my analysis was subject to weekly cancellations.

Fanny and I were quite close. A somewhat older woman, she "mothered" me much as she mothered her younger sisters. Predictably, I was unable to talk to her without complaining about the course of my own analysis. Thus it was that Fanny frequently spoke of me in *her* analysis, especially during those interludes when, as she well knew, Mrs. Deutsch was not seeing me. On one occasion, Fanny told me, she asked Mrs. Deutsch which of us she preferred. Invoking a simile from pathology, Mrs. Deutsch compared the difference between our respective analyses to the difference between dissecting a liver with a rare and complicated condition and dissecting a mere "nutmeg" liver—as if I were a nutmeg liver with only a very ordinary pathology.

From a friend and colleague, Editha Sterba, I later learned Mrs. Deutsch's more pejorative assessment: that I suffered from "paranoid melancholia" and was hence unanalyzable. To me, Mrs. Deutsch mentioned only her own inability to conduct my training analysis, washing her hands of any culpability by appealing to the fact that not even Professor Freud could analyze everyone. By way of bearing out this claim, she mentioned Viktor Tausk, whom Freud had refused to analyze and who later committed suicide after Deutsch, at Freud's direction, dropped him from analysis in 1919. As if further to drive home the Tausk analogy, Mrs. Deutsch made it clear to Fanny von Hann-Kende around this same time that she (Mrs. Deutsch) could not continue to analyze Fanny unless Fanny gave up her relationship to me. Freud, it will be recalled, had instructed Mrs. Deutsch to stop treating Tausk because her preoccupation with him, and constant reflections about him, were interfering with Freud's analysis of her.*

Mrs. Deutsch's uncharitable assessment of me is perhaps less noteworthy than the chain of events set in motion by her summary pronouncement. She herself had received only several months of analysis from Freud and was probably not in a position to understand her countertransference difficulties in working with me. I am inclined to accept the verdict of Lucie

---

*Although I was aggrieved by the publication of Roazen's chronicle of Freud's troubled relationship with Tausk, *Brother Animal* (1969), his verdict is closer to the truth than the vast majority of analysts care to realize.

Jessner, a prominent analyst of the time, that she must have been frightened by my homosexual claims in the transference. I recall a dream I reported in one of our final hours, in which I came out of the bathroom and Mrs. Deutsch, who in the dream was my nurse, buttoned up my underpants (little girls wore underpants with a flap in the back in those days). It was at the end of this hour, be it noted, that Mrs. Deutsch advised me to seek analytic treatment from a man, confessing that she herself could not analyze me.

But the motives behind Mrs. Deutsch's dismissive "diagnosis" notwithstanding, her judgment threw a major roadblock to my psychoanalytic career. Psychoanalytic training at the time was essentially tantamount to a satisfactory training analysis. There was no formal program of study; everyone went a different route, reading, attending seminars, and receiving clinical supervision according to his or her individual circumstances. It was only the training analysis that the candidates had in common, and in terms of graduating from the institute, the judgment of the training analyst about the course of the analysis was decisive. If a training analyst reported to the institute's committee on education that a particular candidate had been successfully analyzed, the committee gave the candidate its stamp of approval without further ado. If, on the other hand, a training analyst testified that a certain candidate had not been, and perhaps could not be, successfully analyzed, then the committee had no recourse but to adjudge that individual unsuitable for psychoanalytic work and to dismiss him or her from the institute.

This is precisely what transpired in my case. Following Mrs. Deutsch's unfavorable report, my fate was, for the time being, sealed. The finality of this verdict was heightened by Helene Deutsch's stature at the time. She was an overpowering personality, and the fact that she had been personally analyzed by Freud, however briefly, rendered her more authoritative still. She wielded great power in the Vienna Psychoanalytic Institute, intimidating a number of male colleagues who had greater analytic experience. Eduard Hitschmann was deadly afraid of her, as was Paul Federn, to a lesser extent. Even Anna Freud took pains not to cross her. Mrs. Deutsch had friendly relationships only with the younger men—Edward Bibring, Ernst Kris, Heinz Hartmann—whom she did not consider professional rivals.

The denouement to her negative evaluation of me was not long in coming. I shortly received a formal letter from Anna Freud, the secretary of the Vienna Psychoanalytic Institute, informing me that I was being dismissed from my "candidate" status. On behalf of the institute, she suggested that I undertake a therapeutic analysis with one of the analysts to whom Mrs. Deutsch had directed me and, if such an analysis proved successful, reapply for admission.

Needless to say, I was crestfallen and quite depressed. At the time Mrs. Deutsch terminated my analysis, I was a guest in the Budapest household of the Kovacs and had the opportunity to discuss my situation on several occasions with Ferenczi. I recall his advice that I resume analytic work with another woman.

He believed that I would have a much easier time with a man, given the fact that I had a much better relationship with my father than with my mother. But for this very reason, Ferenczi held, further work with a woman held the prospect of a much deeper analysis. Mrs. Deutsch herself, at the time of the termination, had suggested three possible analysts to whom I might turn for therapeutic analysis: Willi Hoffer, Richard Sterba, and Edward Bibring. Hoffer, whom I admired, was then unavailable to take me on; he was immersed in study for his medical degree (having already earned his Ph.D.). And I did not wish to approach the other two analysts on the list simply because they were Mrs. Deutsch's choices. And so it was that, flying in the face of the recommendations of the Vienna Psychoanalytic Institute, and ignoring Ferenczi's advice as well, I turned to my mentor and supporter August Aichhorn.

In turning to Aichhorn, I was appealing to an analyst whose own relationship to the Viennese psychoanalytic establishment was anomalous. Aichhorn was definitely a member of the establishment's inner sanctum—and one whose authority was buttressed by his warm friendship with Anna Freud* and privileged status as one of her father's weekly card-playing partners. Yet, at the same time, he remained greatly ambivalent about the institute's hierarchy, rarely attending institute meetings. His distaste for the hierarchy prob-

---

*I believe one of the reasons that Aichhorn took me into analysis—and he almost said as much—was that my profile, and perhaps my eyes or accent as well, reminded him of Anna Freud.

ably had something to do with his own background. Though omnipotent in his own field, he was not an academic, and was always intimidated by academic circles. Beyond this general discomfort, he shared an anxiety more typical of the Hungarians, including Sandor Rado*, for the Viennese hierarchy.

My sorry plight, and the serious depression that accompanied it, was tailor-made for rescue by so magnetic and powerful a personality as Aichhorn. And it played as well into his own distaste for the Viennese establishment. When I presented myself to Aichhorn, he reassured me of my worth and proposed a strategy for gaining my readmittance to the Vienna institute. To wit, he proposed taking me into analysis but suggested that we keep the analysis secret from the members of the institute's committee on education. When he felt we had made sufficient progress, he himself would approach the committee to secure my readmission. Why the secrecy? To know Aichhorn is to intuit the answer. He clearly sought to upstage and upbraid ranking Viennese colleagues toward whom he himself had decidedly mixed feelings. His envisioned scenario, enacted in due course, was that he would confront the institute's committee on education with the fact of our analytic work as a fait accompli and, with grand dra-

---

*Shortly after Rado and I arrived in the United States, he remarked to me in Hungarian that he had believed that studying psychoanalysis in Vienna would be like subjecting himself to the Camarilla, the Austrian secret police who, during Metternich's time, spied on Hungarians.

matic flourish, pronounce it a success: "Her analysis goes excellently; she will be a prominent analyst."

But Aichhorn's seeming relish for a coup over the Viennese establishment hardly detracts from the seriousness of his concern. In fact, his concern, and, more especially, his belief in my aptitude for analytic work, were my salvation during this difficult time. Admittedly, his unorthodox strategy for securing my readmission to the institute also served my narcissistic needs: It bolstered my sense of being a prodigy, a *Wunderkind* destined for important things. And to this extent, my almost three-year analysis with Aichhorn, while helpful in many respects, was far from "classical." For the fact is that Aichhorn and I were, by this time, very much in love with one another, making impossible the classical relationship between analyst and analysand. In taking me under his wing and vowing to see me restored to the good graces of the Viennese psychoanalytic establishment, Aichhorn only buttressed my self-image as an "exception"—now in an entirely positive sense as opposed to the negative sense inculcated by Mrs. Deutsch. Under Aichhorn's analytic care, I became a sort of Cinderella, the love object of a beautiful Prince (Aichhorn) who would win me the favor of a beautiful stepmother (Mrs. Deutsch). At the same time, my analytic treatment with him simply recapitulated my oedipal situation all over again—I was the daughter of both a rejecting mother (Mrs. Deutsch) and a father (Aichhorn) very partial to me.

By the time Aichhorn intervened and secured my readmittance to the institute training program some six

months after our analytic work began, I was his favorite
pupil. As our personal relationship blossomed, I became his lover as well. Realizing, as we both did, that
our work had not been tantamount to the classical
analysis that I still needed, we decided after more than
two-and-a-half years that I should complete my training analysis with someone else. And it was at this juncture that Aichhorn and I jointly decided to ask Willi
Hoffer to analyze me to a successful termination. The
fact that Aichhorn had already secured my admission
to the Vienna Psychoanalytic Institute meant that
Hoffer could work with me completely "above
board," unburdened by any political concerns about
his own status at the institute. And so it was that he
agreed with our judgment that my career would be better served by an analysis with him than by further work
with Aichhorn. Moreover, Hoffer already knew and
liked me, having unofficially supervised the first two
analytic cases that I undertook while still in analysis
with Aichhorn.

Hoffer proved an able training analyst, bringing to
my analysis a much-needed objectivity. Not that he
functioned as a "blank screen" in the manner of
Freud's early technical strictures. We were, as noted,
already fairly good friends and, during the analysis, he
continued to seek my collaboration in the publication
of his new project, the *Journal for Psychoanalytic Pedagogy*. But the fact is that his rapport with me was altogether typical of training analyses of the time, when the
"rule" about keeping the training analyst's private life
out of the analytic work was taken as a guideline rather

than an injunction to be rigidly upheld. My training analysis with Hoffer continued, on and off, until 1935. It was owing to my work with him, I believe, that my character structure, my adaptive skills, and my sublimations all changed for the better.

But the fruits of my analysis with Hoffer notwithstanding, it was as Aichhorn's analysand and pupil that I made great gains, both personal and professional. At the most pedestrian level, it was during my analysis with him that I moved to an apartment at Pfeilgasse 30, a great improvement over my former "dining room" apartment in the Albertgasse. It was Aichhorn who encouraged me to live more comfortably; he persuaded me to purchase a small car, an unheard of luxury at the time, to make my pediatric house calls. At a professional level, it was under Aichhorn's tutelage that I founded my own psychoanalytically oriented well-baby clinic at the outpatient clinic of Professor Zappert; Aichhorn literally mapped out the steps I had to take to secure the necessary authorization. He even urged me to start a child guidance clinic under the auspices of the Vienna Psychoanalytic Institute, a goal that my friend Editha Sterba would later realize.

Aichhorn was similarly responsible for directing me to a new area of clinical endeavor: the use of the Rorschach test as a diagnostic tool. Even before he accepted me as his analysand, he insisted that I learn to interpret Rorschachs because he believed they would aid me in my pediatric work. It was owing to Aichhorn's introduction that I was able to learn Rorschach technique from Behn-Eschenburg, a Swiss pupil of Rorschach himself, when Behn-Eschenburg was visiting Vienna in the late 1920s.

Aichhorn's persistent encouragement about my Rorschach work was well taken and had, as its sequel, my growing expertise in the use of this projective psychological test. In the late 1920s and early thirties, I conducted seminars on Rorschach interpretation for a number of Americans who came to Vienna to study psychoanalysis. These students, who included Margaret Fries, Margaret Ribble, Mary O'Neal Hawkins, and Helen Ross, supplemented their psychoanalytic studies with apprenticeship to Aichhorn to gain a more pragmatic perspective on the therapeutic management of delinquent children. The women spent time in the roving child guidance clinics for which Aichhorn was famous; in addition, Aichhorn referred them to me to learn to use Rorschach tests diagnostically.

My skill in this area stood me in good stead even after I had given up my pediatric practice for full-time work in child analysis. In the early 1930s, I served as a kind of Rorschach expert to the Steinhof psychiatric clinic, a state institution affiliated with the university psychiatric clinic. I was likewise invited to give lectures on the application of the Rorschach test at the university clinic itself, then headed by Pötzl. I should also mention, in passing, one important product of my use of Rorschach tests in clinical practice. Between 1936 and 1938, I collaborated on a research project with Judith Silberpfennig (later Judith Kestenberg) on the significance of the Rorschach in the diagnosis of patients with organic brain damage (organic brain syndrome). Silberpfennig and I administered the Rorschach test to adult patients with "phantom limbs" and found that these patients produced uniformly "anatomical" responses, i.e., responses pertaining to issues of balance, equilibrium, and the symmetry of the body image. The paper that grew out of this project, "The Application of the Rorschach Test to the Psychology of the Organically Brain Damaged," was published in the *Schweitzer Archive für Neurologie und Psychiatrie* in 1938; it has been adjudged a classic by Rorschach experts.

But I am running ahead of my story. To return to the period of my psychoanalytic training: As I began to supplement my pediatric practice with child analytic patients, I was greatly aided by Aichhorn's steady stream of well-paying referrals. At a time when the vast majority of Viennese analysts were struggling to make a living, I was never in need of patients. I must admit that I incurred considerable resentment from colleagues on this score. I recall a time when Berta Bornstein, having recently emigrated from Berlin, was literally starving for want of psychoanalytic patients. She was then more knowledgeable about child analysis than I. And so I asked Aichhorn to send his next analytic case to her rather than to me, to which he replied, "All right, I will do it for you"—he did not particularly care for Berta.

* * *

Perhaps because I was so intent on demonstrating my worth to the entire Viennese psychoanalytic community, I welcomed the opportunity to be supervised in my clinical work by a number of analysts. As I proceeded with my training in the late 1920s, I was supervised at various times by Anna Freud, Jenny Waelder (later Jenny Waelder-Hall), Marianne Kris, Jeanne Lampl-de Groot, Grete Bibring, Eduard Hitschmann, Edward Bibring, and Willi Hoffer. Of these different personalities, several deserve special mention.

Grete Bibring was my first "official" institute-appointed supervisor and, in many ways, the best. A gifted clinician and teacher, she thought highly of my talents and was very encouraging. I recall her supervision of one of my first psychoanalytic patients, a male hairdresser assigned to me by the institute treatment center. He suffered from an anxiety neurosis marked by a fear of women, even though he was simultaneously fascinated with women.

Bibring made a strong impression on me when, in the late 1920s, she gave a talk to the Vienna Psychoanalytic Institute in which she related a strange phenomenon she had observed in herself: she related that when her children were babies, she had perceived and responded to their need for her, even when they were sleeping in other rooms. To speak of the unconscious communication between a nursing mother and her infant was highly unorthodox, if not suspect, at the time; an analyst of less stature than Bibring would not have been taken seriously. But Grete Bibring was listened to, and her talk made a lasting impression on me. I shared her belief in the reality of unconscious communication between nursing mother and infant, that the mother can, via a veritable sixth sense, apprehend when her baby is in distress. This insight would guide me in my own psychoanalytic theory of development, informing my understanding of the early condition of symbiosis between mother and infant.

With respect to treatment issues, it was Grete Bibring who impressed on me the unbelievable distortions that frequently emerge in the analytic transference. She related that one of her patients experienced her as "stupid, lethargic, and fat as a cow"; she was in reality bright as a penny, very energetic, and very thin. I came to understand, under her tutelage, that the analysand will frequently see the analyst as exactly the opposite of what he or she is, that is, as the analysand *needs* to see the analyst.

Willi Hoffer, as noted, unofficially supervised my clinical work before becoming my training analyst. When our friendship threatened to grow into a romantic involvement, he confronted me with the inadvisability of such a development, suggesting that I might in the future need him "in other ways." I recall Hoffer as a good and modest man, unsurpassed in his loyalty to Freud and his daughter, Anna. He was not a brilliant theorist by any means; he liked to refer to himself as a "common soldier" in the psychoanalytic movement. Although he was not as original as, say, Ernst Kris or Heinz Hartmann, he was a very solid citizen throughout his carer. He only came into his own late in life, when he authored several important papers dealing with the development of the body ego, the infant's hand-mouth coordination, and so forth.[1] Some time later, he was elected president of the British Psycho-Analytic Society. His belief in me and his support of my analytic aspirations were instrumental during the period of my training; he was second only to Aichhorn in this respect.

Eduard Hitschmann stands out among my supervisors for the reason that *he* appealed to *me* to place myself in supervision with him. This proved to be an unusual supervision: he spent much of the time complaining about Helene Deutsch's abuse of him, obviously expecting me to lend a sympathetic ear. At a certain point in the supervision, moreover, he asked *me* to teach *him* how to do "defense analysis"—i.e., the analysis of character resistances that was only beginning to become fashionable in the late 1920s, following Freud's publication of *Symptoms, Inhibitions and Anxiety* in 1926.

Of Anna Freud my memories are sparse and unpleasant. I was a member of her child analysis seminar, a continuous case seminar attended by both candidates and members of the Vienna Psychoanalytic Institute. Although she supervised one of my early child analytic cases, I never felt comfortable with her, just as she never felt comfortable with me—but then Anna Freud did not feel comfortable with most people. My own discomfort with her had much to do with her status within the psychoanalytic hierarchy of the time. She, with Helene Deutsch, was the embodiment of "authority" within the movement, the very authority that had thrown such a major obstacle in my path several years earlier. I recall the occasion when I presented my case to Anna Freud at a meeting of the seminar. I presented my material, respectfully listened to her remarks, and virtually ran out of the room!

I have further unpleasant memories associated with the child analysis seminar. At the time I attended the seminar, I was already running the first psychoanalytically oriented well-baby clinic in Vienna. I had founded this clinic, the Ambulatorium Rauscherstrasse, at the suggestion of Professor Zappert, a leading Viennese pediatrician who offerd me the facilities and sponsorship of the Mauthner-Markhoff hospital. This clinic, which preceded the Vienna Institute's own child guidance clinic directed by Editha Sterba, proved the referral source, excepting a few private cases, for the first child patients treated analytically by Viennese child analysts. Thus it was that, although only a candidate of the institute, I was, via my clinic, in a position to refer to my colleagues various cases that were subsequently presented in Anna Freud's child analysis seminar. Jenny Waelder's "Anton," a famous case published in Hoffer's *Journal for Psychoanalytic Pedagogy*, came out of my clinic, for example. Yet, Anna Freud never expressed any appreciation for the abundant material I made available to the seminar members. I recall one occasion when I was curtly informed by one of her lieutenants that Molly Putnam was in Vienna for a short time and that I should furnish her with a case at once. Since the request came to me as a virtual edict, without so much as a perfunctory "please" appended to it, I did not trouble myself to find Molly a case.

Apart from my supervisory relationships and attendance of Anna Freud's child analysis seminar, I had a private tutorial with Robert Waelder on Freud's writings; Aichhorn arranged it during the period of my training analysis with him. I also attended several classes with Edward Bibring that dealt with psychoanalytic instinct theory and Freud's *The Ego and The Id*. I recall Bibring as a good seminar leader and an excellent teacher.

* * *

It was concurrent with my training analysis with Willi Hoffer and participation in Anna Freud's child analytic seminar that I met Paul Mahler. We married in 1936. One of the immediate personal reasons I sought analysis—apart from my desire to become an analyst—involved my relationships with men. I had, throughout my early adulthood, been courted by a number of exceptional academics: *privatdozents,* professors, and the like. Yet, my father remained adamant in his belief that marriage, and the acceptance of femininity that it entailed, were not for me. Whenever I returned to Sopron and informed my family of a new suitor, he would offer an admonishment that became a virtual refrain. Why did I need to marry, he would ask, when I was so self-sufficient? I was really much "better" than the average man. Moreover, he continued, my sister Suzanne was much less self-sufficient than I and, given the uncertainties of her own life, she would always need me to "be there" for her. Thus the frustrating familial missions with which I was burdened.

Although I understood my father's attitude to be

both unnatural and selfish, it nonetheless exerted a strong influence on my attitude toward men, and on my array of promising suitors in particular. Owing to my father, I came to believe that my "superiority" was such that I could never really be "feminine" enough or "submissive" enough to marry. In fact, I came to believe that any man who became devoted to me must be my "inferior." And, on the basis of this belief, I undoubtedly gave subtle cues that discouraged my many suitors. At my very first interview with Helene Deutsch, I recall relating to her my awareness of always running away from men just when a relationship reached a degree of seriousness that seemed to invite a proposal. It was at the very point in a relationship at which I realized that I could indeed attract men to whom I felt reciprocally attracted, in other words, that I felt I was dealing with an "inferior" with whom I best not proceed further.

It was in the context of wrestling with this issue in my analysis with Hoffer that I met Paul Mahler, a very cultured and gentle man who was not a professor at all, but rather a chemist—albeit one with a Ph.D. and a wonderfully rich classical education as well. Although the junior partner of a Viennese cordial factory begun by his late father and his father's living brother, he was far from successful. He had put his entire inheritance into the factory, feeling obliged to match the investment of his much wealthier uncle. But these investments notwithstanding, the factory continued to lose money year after year. In fact, the factory's prospects were so poor that, prior to our marriage, Paul elected to relinquish his share in it entirely and simply manage the business on a fixed salary.

As I look back, I see my marriage to Paul Mahler at the age of thirty-nine as a pseudosolution to psychological problems that were still not fully resolved. Paul was an only son who had been very attached both to his father and his mother. He told me that when he once expressed the desire to seek employment outside of Vienna—in Turin, to be specific—his father had reacted tearfully, making Paul feel that he simply "could not do that" to him. In marrying Paul, I was choosing to marry a man very unlike my father, in fact, a man who very much needed, in his adult life, both a mother and a father. This neediness on his part made for a marriage that was far from easy. Although he was tremendously proud of me and openly expressed his pride to other people, he tried to ward off his admiration in our private life at the same time as he refused to be protective of me or to assume the dominant role in the marriage in general.

In later years, our respective professional circumstances played a role in our personal relationship. At the time of our marriage in 1936, I was already successful. And I would become more successful still following our emigration to America in 1938, the currency of psychoanalysis in America and the special prestige of European-trained analysts undoubtedly helping me along. Paul, on the other hand, had a series of low-paying chemical jobs far below his competence, ultimately ending up with a generally adequate, but still low-paying job with the Geigy Corporation.[2]

* * *

As I reflect back on my experience in Vienna, I associate to an incident from early childhood. When I was about ten years old, Emma Toppler, the daughter of the mayor of Sopron, had a party. Although she did not initially invite me, my father, without my knowledge, spoke with her father, the Bürgermeister. A liveried servant arrived at our apartment shortly thereafter with my formal invitation. At the party, the table was covered with a large tablecloth; Emma autographed it and then invited the other children, some thirteen or fourteen in all, to do likewise. But she and her other guests prevented me from adding my name to the tablecloth.

In many ways, the years of my psychoanalytic training are encapsulated in this painful childhood memory. In Vienna, too, I was accepted and yet unaccepted, present at the party and yet excluded from the coterie of privileged guests. The Viennese psychoanalytic world was always divided into "insiders" and "outsiders." Anyone who had a personal relationship with, or had been analyzed by, Freud was considered one of the specially chosen. Annie Angel (later Annie Katan); Marianne Kris; Helene Deutsch; and, of course, Anna Freud were prominent among these insiders during the 1920s and thirties; they were viewed as authority figures, their every word pregnant with the weight and authority of Freud.

My position in Vienna was anomalous. Within the analytic establishment, I was clearly an outsider, a member of the Budapest circle whose initial training analysis with Helene Deutsch had run aground. And yet, I achieved a status which, if not privileged, certainly made for a type of grudging acceptance. A favorite of Aichhorn, I had the run of his famous network of child guidance clinics. While under his tutelage, I not only became an expert in the clinical use of Rorschach tests, but assumed the direction of the well-baby clinic that furnished the members of Anna Freud's child analysis seminar with much of their case material. While all this was happening, I was an established pediatrician entrusted with the care of the children of many analysts,[3] not to mention the children of other prominent members of the Vienna medical community, including Beno Samet, the ranking internist who cared for Freud in Max Schur's absence. In short, I was accepted and yet unaccepted, just as I had been accepted and unaccepted at the childhood party of Emma Toppler.

As I contemplate the grounds for the continuing "outsider" status that accompanied my many professional accomplishments in Vienna, I harken back to my own resistance to one of the major requirements for "insider" status: I refer to my rebellion against the sterile atmosphere that pervaded the Vienna Psychoanalytic Institute during this time. This was the period in which Freud's strictures about analytic "neutrality" were literally taken as a mandate for a therapeutic attitude of utter detachment.[4] In the Vienna of the 1920s and early thirties, it was anathema even to speak about analysis with emotion, much less to infuse one's therapeutic work with emotion. A good analyst, an "insider" analyst, could not show *any* emotion under *any* circumstances. I recall a brief conversation with Anna Freud that highlights this aspect of the prevailing psychoanalytic ethos. We were discussing a colleague, Clara Frankel, who was highly regarded for her work with psychotics. It was common knowledge that psychotics under her care made great progress and were eventually able to leave the state institutions where they had been long confined. When I remarked that Frankel was wonderful with her psychotic patients, Anna Freud demurred, opining that therapeutic skill with psychotics had nothing to do with psychoanalysis or with one's psychoanalytic competence.

This ethos of antiseptic detachment from patient care prescribed by the Vienna Psychoanalytic Institute ran counter to everything I had learned and experienced as a pediatrician. I had seen, in von Pirquet's clinic, how devastating a sterile, detached approach to sick children could be; conversely, I had seen in Moll's institute how therapeutically potent an approach of loving engagement could be with equally sick children. In my future work, I would elaborate a theory of early development and a therapeutic perspective that sought to do justice to both of these competing emphases, to what I understood of the technical requirements of psychoanalytic work and to what I had learned as a pediatrician of the emotional requirements of early life.

In 1933, the period of my formal psychoanalytic training came to a close when I was certified by the committee on education of the Vienna Psychoanalytic Institute. But even this final vindication was incomplete, shorn of the privileged "insider" status for which I longed. I learned from Editha Sterba that my acceptance by the committee would have been unanimous but for one dissenting vote—that of Helene Deutsch.

Nineteen thirty-three, the year of my official acceptance as an analyst, was also the year of Ferenczi's death. Along with many members of the Viennese psychoanalytic community, I journeyed to Budapest to attend the funeral of the man who had steered me to a psychoanalytic career and been my steadfast advocate during the decade of my training. Ironically, I travelled to the funeral of my patron and friend on the same train as the woman how had exerted herself to derail my budding career. Helene Deutsch and I said nothing to one another during the sad journey.

5 · Sea Change

The Anschluss of 1938, by which Nazi Germany annexed Austria, was merely the final step in the sad deterioration of Austrian political life throughout the 1930s. Within two months of Hitler's occupation of the country in March 1938, virtually the entire Austrian psychoanalytic community had departed for Britain or America. It is perhaps ironic that the eminent Hungarian sculptor, Beni Ferenczy, a friend whose children were under my pediatric care, finished his bust of me on the very eve of the *Umbruch*—the night before the Austrian chancellor Kurt Schuschnigg quietly left Vienna for Berchtesgaden, where he would capitulate completely to Hitler's demands and, in so doing, extinguish the last glowing ember of Austrian independence.

In point of fact, I had contemplated leaving Austria years before the fateful events of 1938. The rise of Nazism in the 1930s, which brought in its wake a whole series of putsches and the assassination of Chancellor Dollfuss in 1934, was never remote from the personal and professional lives of both me and my husband, Paul. During the late thirties, Aichhorn, ever the "insider" with reliable information about police activities, would call me on certain mornings and warn me not to let my husband brave the streets to get to the Mahler factory, owing to the daily quota of Jews to be rounded up by the police in the Josefstadt district in which we resided. "Listen," he would tell me, "a contingent of fifty Jews is to be rounded up in the Josefstadt today; don't let your husband go to his plant." Daily reports of those actually arrested led me to take

Aichhorn's advice to heart, although I had my hands full keeping Paul at home on those days when Aichhorn felt it unwise for him to venture onto the streets. In opting for the safety of our apartment, Paul always felt he was letting down the elderly uncle with whom he managed the family business.

The political situation, and especially the worsening plight of Jews, naturally had a great impact on psychoanalytic work during this time. I have one especially salient memory of a man, a non-Jew, who was in analysis because of a potency disturbance. He was employed by Siemens Schukert, the largest armory factory in Austria. I knew he would not be able to continue with treatment in the deteriorating political climate and, sure enough, he came to his session following one weekend and announced, "Of course, you will understand that I cannot come because I have a little bit of Jewish blood in me, am therefore distrusted, and am followed to your office every day." Obviously feeling some remorse on my behalf, he proceeded to ask if there was anything he could do for me.

Before completing this story, I must interject a piece of personal history. Some years earlier, the first wife of the sculptor Ferenczy whose children, as noted, were under my care, asked me if I could use some second-hand baby clothing for the poor charges at my well-baby clinic. I was happy to accept her offer, and she thereupon brought me a large bundle of her children's used clothing. In between two pieces of clothing I discovered, to my amazement, a revolver. The woman presumably wanted to get rid of it, along with the clothing, prior to emigrating to Russia. I was, to say the least, uncomfortable with this "gift" but chose simply to put it aside for the time being.

The rest of my story now falls into place. When my patient, full of warnings about the fate of Jews and others of whom the Nazis did not approve, asked if he could do me a favor, I immediately thought of "my" revolver. It occurred to me that, as an employee of an ammunition factory, he must certainly have a gun permit, but I put the question to him nonetheless. When he answered affirmatively, I explained that I happened to have a revolver, but no permit, and had heretofore been unable to dispose of the weapon. I then asked him outright if he would simply take the weapon and do with it whatever he wished. When he said he would, I got out the revolver and gave it to him. He took the weapon, inspected it, and remarked, "This is a beautiful piece, a beautiful piece, but it has a small imperfection. It does not work, but it's a small matter to fix it." Need I add that this man had come for analysis because he suffered from ejaculatio praecox?

So events both inside and outside my practice convinced me well before the Anschluss that we should make plans to emigrate. As early as January 1937, I approached my husband's uncle, a spa doctor in the Sudeten part of Germany, near Karlsbad, about my desire to leave the country. He reminded me that we would need affidavits to leave Austria but made light of my appeal by offering his opinion that the Nazis were, in early 1937, "whistling at their last hole." How ironic that this dismissive remark came from an

Margaret Mahler, ca. 1940, a year or so after arriving in the United States. *(Photograph by Trude Fleischmann.)*

Left, Caroline Zachry, who founded the Zachry Institute of Human Development in 1939 and, from 1942 to her death in 1945, served as director of the Bureau of Child Guidance of the New York City Board of Education, befriended Margaret Mahler soon after Mahler arrived in the United States in the fall of 1938. In addition to appointing Mahler to the staff of her institute, she introduced her to the pediatrician Benjamin Spock. *(From the Estate of Margaret S. Mahler.)*

Right and below: Mahler relaxing in Brookfield, Connecticut, in 1945. This was the summer she learned that her mother had been deported and murdered in Auschwitz. *(From the Estate of Margaret S. Mahler.)*

Mahler ca. 1950, when she joined the staff of the recently founded Albert Einstein College of Medicine and accepted the chairmanship of the child analysis training program of the Philadelphia Psychoanalytic Institute. *(From the Estate of Margaret S. Mahler.)*

Top: In this photo of 1952, Mahler stands between two influential teachers and colleagues, Anna Freud (left) and Grete Bibring (right), at the 17th Congress of the International Psychoanalytic Association in Amsterdam. It was on this occasion that Mahler presented her celebrated paper, "On Child Psychosis and Schizophrenia: Autistic and Symbiotic Infantile Psychoses," subsequently published in volume 7 of *The Psychoanalytic Study of the Child*. *(From the Estate of Margaret S. Mahler.)* Bottom: Mahler is honored on the publication of the festschrift *Separation-Individuation: Essays in Honor of Margaret S. Mahler,* edited by John B. McDevitt and Calvin F. Settlage, in 1971. She is flanked by Judith Kestenberg, Abram Kagan (publisher of International Universities Press), and Selma Kramer. *(From the Estate of Margaret S. Mahler.)*

Mahler with Selma Kramer and Leo Madow at the 1977 Margaret S. Mahler Symposium in Philadelphia. The annual symposia, sponsored jointly by the Medical College of Pennsylvania and the Philadelphia Psychoanalytic Society and Institute, began in 1969 and continue into the present. (*From the files of the Medical College of Pennsylvania.*)

Mahler, on being honored by the United Jewish Appeal–Federation of Jewish Philanthropies, January 18, 1976. (*Photograph by Jerry Soalt.*)

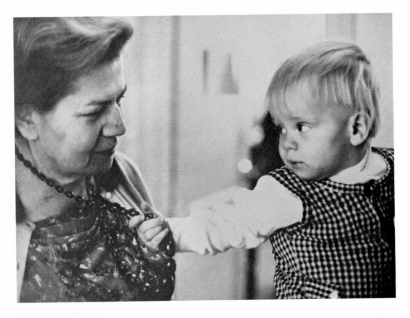

This photo of 1967, a still frame from the extensive collection of research films documenting the separation-individuation process, was one of Mahler's personal favorites. *(From the Margaret S. Mahler Psychiatric Research Foundation.)*

Mahler in 1975, the year *The Psychological Birth of the Human Infant* was published. *(From the Margaret S. Mahler Psychiatric Research Foundation.)*

Top: Mahler in her eighties. *(From the Estate of Margaret S. Mahler.)* Bottom: Some eight years before her death, Mahler arranged to have her own ashes and those of her late husband, Paul H. Mahler, transported to Sopron and interred in the Jewish cemetery next to the grave of her father. At the same time, Mahler arranged to have her mother's name engraved on her father's tombstone, prefaced by the words "Martyr of the Holocaust." These wishes were fulfilled in August 1986. *(From the Estate of Margaret S. Mahler.)*

inhabitant of the Sudetenland, the part of Austria that the Nazis would first swallow.

Of course, the events of 1937 and 1938 entirely justified my apprehensions. I recall the great panic that overtook many Viennese Jewish intellectuals at the time the Nazi troops moved into Austria in March 1938. The Viennese analysts, while naturally sharing in the heightened concern, were less panicked by the political turn of events than other professionals. In fact, they really behaved in a quite "analyzed" way, banding together in the tradition of the most efficient Freemason groups and undertaking systematic organizational work to see to it that every Jewish analyst was safely relocated. I recall attending a conference at the time at Freud's home, chaired by Anna Freud and attended by the most influential and well-connected analysts—the Bibrings, Ernst Kris, and Heinz Hartmann, among others. The point of the gathering was to plot the relocation of Jewish analysts outside of Austria and to take steps to procure affidavits and visas for those who would shortly be leaving. I recall that, at one point during this meeting, it was proposed that Paul and I be assigned to South Africa—a suggestion that Grete Bibring joined us in heartily opposing!

Along with many colleagues, we sought temporary asylum in Britain and, in our case, this wish was fulfilled through the good offices of Leontine Sassoon, widow of the British Viceroy of India. I then had Lady Sassoon's niece in analysis, and Lady Sassoon not only sent a letter on our behalf to the Viennese Home Office of the British Embassy, asking that we be granted emigration visas, but even invited me and my husband to stay with her pending our subsequent emigration to the United States. Armed with this letter, we went to the British Consulate and asked for a three-month visa. To our surprise, and owing, no doubt, to Lady Sassoon's influential sponsorship, we were granted six months in Britain and were further granted authorization to prepay our passage from Britain to New York.

We had just enough money to conclude our affairs in Vienna, which included substantial taxes on my husband's factory,* and to purchase the tickets for the boat trip from Southampton to New York that would follow our brief sojourn in Britain. On the eve of our departure from Vienna, Paul and I had one and a half guineas each to our names. Fortunately, I happened to have a cousin in Yugoslavia with money in Switzerland who had indicated he would wire us funds once we were out of Austria. The Hungarian government, for its part, granted my parents a one-day permit that enabled them to travel to Vienna—where they could say good-bye to us—and return to Hungary within a day. For me it was an utterly excruciating farewell. I sat in my mother's lap and clung to her like a baby—like the baby I had never been allowed to be. At the same time, I recall feeling that perhaps it was my mother who would be unable to survive without *me*, so totally had

---

*Jews were not permitted simply to leave Austria. They had to pay taxes not only for themselves, but for those who, on account of their departure, might be lost to the economy. I had to draw on my savings to pay this so-called Reich emigration tax (*Reichsfluchtsteuer*) for the employees of Paul's company.

our roles become reversed over the years. For the same mother who had never taken me to her as a child, her child, had herself become an increasingly helpless child over the years, suffering greatly from severe rheumatoid arthritis and in constant need of "maternal" support from her elder daughter.

My five-month stay in Britain, from May through October of 1938, was a period of happy reunion with former Viennese colleagues, especially the Bibrings and the Krisses. The British Psycho-Analytic Society was very generous to the European émigré analysts, especially the Viennese. It paid for our residence at Greencroft Gardens (Hampstead), where we lived in a boarding house owned and managed by Hedwig Abraham, widow of the German analyst Karl Abraham. In fact, the British Psycho-Analytic Society was very accommodating in all respects, albeit with the understanding that the vast majority of émigrés were "in transit" and would not be relocating permanently in Britain.

I was the only psychoanalyst living at Greencroft Gardens at this time, although the novelist (and Freud's later correspondent) Arnold Zweig and his wife were also among Mrs. Abraham's temporary tenants. At the boarding house, Mrs. Abraham, whom I had not formerly met, proved a very efficient if somewhat domineering landlady. With the Abrahams' only daughter, Hilda, who lived with her mother, I became very friendly. I recall discussing Hilda with Mrs. Abraham, especially the fact that she had never married. These discussions were prompted by our joint reading and discussion of a paper by Abraham that dealt with masturbation and was published some time after his death. I recall being astonished at how punitively Abraham spoke about masturbation.[1]

It was while living at Greencroft Gardens in 1938 that I received a final gift from my mother. She had taken her set of diamond earrings and had them made into a set of matching rings—one for me and one for my sister. My ring, interestingly enough, was delivered to me at Mrs. Abraham's boarding house by the husband of the British analyst, Melanie Klein.

My brief stay in Britain went quickly owing to the variety of personal and professional activities that consumed all my waking hours. Many of my days, and some of my husband's as well, were spent at Woburn House, trying to rescue colleagues, friends, and family still in Vienna; I helped get my husband's family to London. I recall attending many seminars in nearby Hampstead, including those directed by Anna Freud and Susan Isaacs; the latter was especially interested in bringing all the émigré analysts under one roof so the work of analysis could go forward. I paid several visits to Anna Freud and recall, at my farewell visit, seeing her father bid farewell to Stefan Zweig, who was also leaving the country. Paul, for his part, studied Rorschach interpretation and English when he was not working to expedite the emigration of family and friends. We socialized with my former Viennese colleagues, especially the Krisses and the Bibrings.

I managed to continue with professional work during this period as well. Since I wanted to "earn my keep" and not be entirely dependent on the generosity of the British Psycho-Analytic Society, I administered Rorschach tests and spent much additional time informally teaching Rorschach technique—everyone wanted to learn Rorschach in those days. I had several paying patients as well. Lady Sassoon's niece and two other adolescent patients followed me to Britain to continue their treatment. Another colleague from Vienna, Hilda Maas, who arrived in Britain sometime before I did, gave me the use of her office to see these patients. At the same time, she referred to me her own son, Heino, perhaps eight years of age, who was then experiencing some early school-age difficulties. Among his symptoms was his "pretending" not to understand German, his native tongue, teamed with his willingness to converse only in English. In the course of our brief psychotherapy, I discovered that Heino's symptom was tied to his relationship with his mother, of whom he repeatedly said, "she takes away my words." At one of his mother's cocktail parties that I attended, a guest asked the child a question to which his mother, ignoring Heino, immediately gave reply. Turning to me, Heino remarked, "You see what I mean when I say that she takes away my words?" In fact, this little boy proved my first and most effective English teacher. Of all the Viennese émigré analysts, I probably knew the least English on arriving in Britain. It was through the psychotherapy with Heino that I mastered what basic English I had on arriving in the United States. Sensitized to language by the mother who unwittingly "took away [his] words," he was quick to come to my rescue whenever I had difficulty expressing myself in English.

It was without great happiness that I planned for my departure to America. The prospect of journeying there had always been intimidating for me. Years earlier, von Pirquet had offered to get me a Carnegie Fellowship through which I could spend 1923–24 in America, but I did not encourage his initiative. I would not have been intimidated by a fellowship that provided for work in France or anywhere else in Europe. But America? It was so far away, and the prospect of going there was very frightening. Only the Nazis could have sent me there.

In Britain, I was much nearer to my parents than I would be in America, and the magnitude of crossing the ocean and resettling in an environment in which I would have neither friends nor professional contacts was rather overwhelming. Since the British Home Office had extended our visas from three to six months, our friends and colleagues had enough time to expedite the paperwork that would make our departure possible. Our affidavits for emigration to the United States were especially expedited by Esther and William Menaker of New York; the Menakers were very helpful in obtaining affidavits for a great many Viennese analysts during this difficult time. But even after the affidavits arrived, we still needed visas to enter the country. In obtaining these latter documents, we were indebted to Dorothy Burlingham, who wrote Joseph Kennedy, the American ambassador to Britain, asking him to intercede and speed up the processing of our applications.

Paul and I left Britain almost as penniless as we had arrived. I must mention Ernest Jones's generosity in this regard. Although I may have met Jones once in Vienna, I only got to know him in Britain, where we attended several parties together. (It was at one such party that I met Melanie Klein.) When Jones learned of our imminent departure, he invited me to his Harley Street office, where he asked me directly how much money we would have on disembarking in the United States. I replied with candor that we had 10 or maybe 15 pounds, but that we had prepaid our passage on the Queen Mary. I also mentioned the cousin in Yugoslavia who had promised to send us money from Switzerland on our arrival. But these remarks did nothing to allay Jones's anxiety on our behalf. "Dr. Mahler," he announced, "you cannot disembark in New York with 10 or 15 pounds. You will accept this 500 guineas as a loan from the British Psycho-Analytic Society, and you will not disembark without it." By way of explanation, Jones added that, whereas we might not need this money in order to survive, it would nonetheless look very, very bad if we arrived in the United States without money. Jones's implication was clear: an analyst simply did not come to America penniless, a veritable member of the proletariat! He expressed his certainty that we would pay back the money as soon as we were able—which we did. I reminded Jones of this loan when he came to America in 1956 to participate in the centenary celebration of Freud's birth. But Jones was a gentleman and would hear nothing of it in public.

Paul and I set sail for the United States on the Queen Mary in October of 1938. There were no other analysts on board. When, shortly after arriving in New York, I wrote a friend about the journey, I characterized the ship as *traumhaft* ("dreamlike," "beautiful"), adding that "she rocks a lot." The latter recollection was perhaps the more telling, since I recall being seasick the entire trip. I also recall being eager to see the Statue of Liberty and asking my husband to see to it that I did not miss her when we approached New York harbor. I vaguely recall my feelings on seeing the statute: very romantic feelings about liberty that would linger with me over the course of my life. Likewise, I am still strangely uplifted on seeing the Union Jack or hearing the "Star Spangled Banner." At the time of our arrival, these symbols were all the more powerful owing to their contrast with the terrifying swastikas that seemed to be smeared all over Vienna during the several weeks that preceded our departure.

Several of my colleagues met Paul and me at the dock; Bertha Bornstein was the first to greet us. These and other colleagues, many of whom had arrived in the United States just several weeks before us, were kind enough to get us a room in the Hotel Paris, then quite elegant, and to send us a basket of beautiful fruit that I greatly enjoyed. Among those who befriended us at the time of our arrival were Margaret Ribble, at whose home in Provincetown we spent our first summer, and Dr. and Mrs. Leo Stone.

Of course, our stay at the Hotel Paris was, in the nature of things, quite temporary, and Paul lost no time in searching for an apartment where we could live. But we naturally had no idea about what was *comme il faut* in New York; to wit, we did not know that West

96th Street was, and still is, a dividing line separating that portion of Manhattan where aspiring professionals (in our case, a chemist and a would-be psychoanalyst) may live from that portion where they may not. It was owing to this inevitable ignorance that we ended up in a beautiful new apartment house on 98th Street and Columbus Avenue. I recall that it was a walk-up furnished with handsome maple furniture—our furniture from Europe had not yet arrived—and seemed quite spacious after our cramped hotel room.

But it was not long before we realized that this lovely apartment was on the wrong side of the dividing line and, as a professional address, simply would not do. The first two patients whom, with great trepidation, I took on at this address, both had multiple dreams, the latent meaning of which revolved around their condescension toward me and pity for me, owing especially to the location of my apartment! To make matters worse, it slowly dawned on us that we were not receiving our mail. Edith Buxbaum, who had been in America for quite some time preceding our arrival, had allowed us to use her address in the east seventies as our mailing address at the time of our arrival. But her secretary had been unwittingly, and routinely, forwarding our mail to West 89th Street rather than West 98th; the mail never reached us.

And so for various reasons we stayed in our 98th Street apartment only several months. By the time Paul resumed his search for new lodgings, we understood that most of the refugee analysts lived on Central Part West or thereabouts, so Paul went from building to building on this street. And he found us a one-room apartment in the very beautiful and very prestigious building at 336. It was the building where Ruth Loveland, the well-known American analyst, lived. Of course, by this time I had learned my lesson well. I would have scrimped on our food budget before I compromised on the address of our new apartment!

I reserve the story of my early professional struggles in New York for the next chapter but cannot conclude this brief account of my relocation without mentioning an incident that shortly followed our move to 336 Central Park West. The relevant background to this event is as follows: Shortly after arriving in the United States, I was befriended by Dr. Caroline Zachry, then Director of the Institute of Human Development, head of the Bureau of Child Guidance of the New York City Board of Education, and a close friend of the pediatrician Benjamin Spock. Following Zachry's introduction, Ben Spock and I became good friends over the summer of 1939, and when he learned that I was rather knowledgeable about the emotional disturbances of children, he used to come to visit me, always bringing a large stack of charts so that we could discuss the emotional problems of his patients. It was Spock, then in analysis with Bertram Lewin, who referred to me my first child analytic patients following my arrival. I recall the very first child he sent to me, a little boy with encopresis.

When Paul and I moved into 336 Central Park West, we received several strange and apparently crank phone calls. On one such occasion, I was asked whether the callers could bring a little girl to the apartment to be circumcised. I became sufficiently frightened by this call that I immediately asked my husband to get us an unlisted phone number.

Now, the humorous incident in question: On one of the hottest days of August during my first summer in New York, our apartment bell rang. Feeling greatly oppressed with the heat and humidity of my first August in New York, I answered the door very scantily dressed. And there stood Ben Spock, a towering figure of well over six feet. "Margaret," he said, "I'm so glad you are all right. I left my patients. I was in the middle of office hours, but I couldn't get you on the phone and wanted to make sure you were all right." I have never forgotten this touching gesture.

6 • First Years in America

The New York psychoanalytic establishment offered the newly arrived refugees a reception that was ambivalent if not double-edged. Given the realities of psychoanalytic practice, including the limited population of potential analysands, many senior analysts were less than sympathetic to the avalanche of rather prestigious European analysts who were then concentrated in New York. While nominally sympathetic to the plight of the refugees and helpful in expediting their relocation, these establishment figures made it plain that they would be happier if their European colleagues sank roots outside the boroughs of New York City.

This was the outcome of a famous conference chaired by Adolph Stern, then chairman of the Educational Committee of the New York Psychoanalytic Society, and attended by most of the refugee analysts in 1939.* Senior New York analysts, especially Stern, Lawrence Kubie, and Sandor Rado, advised us to get our New York medical licenses and then go "pioneering" to Buffalo, Utica, Syracuse, or some other upstate location. They also impressed upon us that, now in America, we refugees must respect the sanctity of the American medical profession and its hold on psychoanalysis: we must not undertake any analytic work until we obtained our medical licenses.[1]

I, along with many others at the meeting, was too stunned at the time to reply to this directive to leave

---

*Ludwig Jekels and Edith Jacobson were the only "exceptions" made by the analytic establishment. It was understood that they would remain in New York City and, accordingly, they were not asked to attend the conference.

the city. But others, like Annie Reich, were quick to articulate our indignation at this preposterous request. Many of us—including me—spoke so little English that we could never hope to be understood by the "common man."* How could we go pioneering in Buffalo? Shortly after this conference, my husband, Paul, landed a job with a manufacturer in Elizabeth, New Jersey. On learning of this development, Lawrence Kubie invited me to lunch and, in his saccharin manner, tried to sell me on the idea of establishing myself there: "Dr. Mahler, the best possible solution would be for you to go to Elizabeth. It is only a few minutes from New York, you know." I naturally declined this invitation.[2]

With respect to surmounting the hurdle of obtaining a New York State medical license, I was more fortunate than most of my fellow refugees. Although I had to repeat the English examination a second time—Mrs. Leo Stone helped me greatly with my language skills—I passed the state medical board on the first try and

---

*It is an interesting footnote to my own language difficulties that, on top of my self-consciousness about my limited English at the time, I was berated by certain Hungarian colleagues for speaking English with a heavy Viennese accent. Several weeks after we arrived in the United States, I was invited to discuss a paper presented at a meeting of the American Hungarian Medical Association. I believe I did a very good job but will never forget the aftermath of my remarks. When the meeting was over, I went to a salon where my female colleagues confronted me and exclaimed: "What an awful Viennese accent you have!" It wasn't Hungarian enough for them and, for quite some time, my Hungarian colleagues in this country considered me a virtual renegade!

received my license near the end of 1939. Actually, I was a single point shy of a passing score in two areas, gynecology and anatomy. When I appealed in writing to the state board, however, it saw fit to accept my scores and grant me the medical and surgical license. Interestingly, the relative ease with which I obtained my license filled me with guilt rather than elation. Specifically, I felt bad thinking of those European colleagues who absolutely needed their licenses in order to practice and earn a living. I think especially of my Viennese colleagues the Waltuchs—he an internist and she a pediatrician—who both flunked the examination on the very occasion that I passed it. So my triumph on this score was tempered by pangs of guilt.

But I was, by this time, already preoccupied with the New York psychoanalytic scene, and especially the malevolent quarrels besetting it. To me, a refugee for whom Hitler and the swastika were parts of the immediate past, these quarrels and splits were upsetting, and all the more so owing to their malignant, underhanded quality. I never understood the widespread animosity toward Clara Thompson and Karen Horney, as no one cared to enlighten me as to the details of their situation.

With respect to the splitting of the New York Psychoanalytic Society into rival factions, I innocently became a pawn when, in 1940, Lawrence Kubie assigned me the task of giving the child analysis seminar, effectively, if only temporarily, making me the society's senior teacher of child analysis. Up to that time, the entire child analytic field had been in the hands of David M.

Levy, a creative thinker and gifted researcher for whom
I had great admiration. Kubie, for political reasons unknown to me at the time, wanted Levy out, just as he
wanted Rado out, Thompson out, and Horney out.
But Kubie, adroit power broker that he was, did not
engineer the dethronement of his rivals heavy hand-
edly; rather, he implemented his designs subtly and
skillfully, "with much vaseline," as my teacher Aichhorn used to say. And so it was that I became a pawn
in his plot to remove David Levy from authority in the
field of child analysis. I was given responsibility for the
child analysis seminar largely by default: I was politically acceptable to Kubie and, among the European
child analysts, no one else was then available who was
both an M.D. and had received the New York State
license—the Krisses had not yet arrived. Levy, it should
be noted, took my appointment as a terrible slight; he
subsequently resigned from both the New York Psychoanalytic Society and the American Psychoanalytic
Association.

Apart from the New York Psychoanalytic Society,
my first institutional anchorage came by way of Caroline Zachry's Institute of Human Development, where
I joined my friend Ben Spock and a host of distinguished educators and psychologists as a nonsalaried
member of the staff. The institute was something of a
"think tank" that served as the parent organization of
the Educational Institute, headed by Edith T. Schmidt.
Both the Institute of Human Development and the
Educational Institute were active in the realm of what
Europeans call *Heilpädagogik*, which is to say remedial

teaching of children with emotional disturbances and learning disabilities. The Educational Institute provided the actual services for these children.

I was welcomed on the staff of the Institute of Human Development not only as a Viennese-trained analyst, but as a Rorschach expert who had learned Rorschach interpretation from Behn-Eschenburg, a pupil of Rorschach himself. Rorschach testing was then considered an important evaluative tool in work with disturbed children, and Klopfer, the American Rorschach expert, was on the staff of the institute.

I have already mentioned that Caroline Zachry not only befriended me soon after my arrival in this country, but introduced me to Ben Spock. Here I should add that my friendship with her, which began at the time I was appointed to the institute staff, put me in the highly awkward position of being asked by her to work analytically with her adopted son. I say "awkward" because the request for intervention came from the child's school, and his mother, as head of the Bureau of Child Guidance of the New York City Board of Education, was predictably miffed at the request; she refused to believe that *her* son could be in need of treatment. So she asked me to help, then withdrew the request, which was made a second time by the principal of her son's school, which Dr. Zachry then went along with. I worked with the child for a time, but it was an extremely ticklish situation for all parties concerned.

My formal acceptance into the New York Psychoanalytic Society followed my presentation on "Pseudoimbecility: A Magic Cap of Invisibility" in January 1940. I had agreed to make this topic my maiden presentation before the Christmas holidays of 1939 but then, in a somewhat reckless way, accepted the invitation of a friend to spend the vacation period in Florida, thereby postponing the actual writing of the paper. My husband, Paul, who did not wish to disturb my rest, waited until my return to present me with the formal announcement of my presentation later in January. So, with some trepidation, I set about writing the paper, which I then showed to Annie Reich, whom I greatly admired and whose judgment I greatly respected. Annie was very critical of this first draft, so I returned to the drawing board and wrote another version from scratch. This second draft elicited her high praise, and it was this version that was delivered to my colleagues shortly thereafter. The basic idea of this paper was that certain children appear "dumb" (and indeed *have* to appear dumb) in order to disguise their sexual enlightenment. Among the discussants of the presentation, David Levy, I recall, was critical. He later wrote me a complimentary letter, however, professing that he had misunderstood my thesis at the time of the presentation but, on reflection and rereading, had become convinced that I was essentially right in what I was saying.

My presentation of January 1940 had several happy outcomes. I immediately became a member of the New York Psychoanalytic Society. Moreover, the *Psychoanalytic Quarterly* immediately requested and subsequently published my lecture.[3] Finally, a colleague, Dr.

Lillian Kaplan, who was greatly impressed with the presentation, "sold me," so to speak, to the New York State Psychiatric Institute, affiliated with Columbia University. She represented me to the powers-that-be as a refugee child analyst who could perhaps bring some order to the children's service of the institute.

So it was that, immediately following my lecture, I was invited by Dr. Kaplan, on behalf of Dr. Lillian Powers, to become the nonsalaried chief consultant to the children's service of the New York State Psychiatric Institute. I was simultaneously offered, in this same context, an appointment as an Associate in Psychiatry at Columbia University. The children's service had long been a poor-sister adjunct to the adult service of the Psychiatric Institute; when the institute was founded, the planners seemingly forgot that provisions would have to be made for the treatment of children. As a result, the latter never had a paid chief; it traditionally leaned on, and borrowed personnel from, the adult service. Nonetheless, it was in the children's service of the institute that I found the most marvelous clinical material, which, owing to the lowly (and unbudgeted) status of the children's service, I was free to work with as I saw fit.

This exhilarating freedom contrasted favorably with my brief prior experience in the children's outpatient department of Mount Sinai Hospital where, along with Annie Reich and several other refugees, I had been invited by Lawrence Kubie. Kubie's arbitrary directorial powers, including his dictatorial control of the

clinical conferences, was anathema to me; it was remi-
niscent of the stifling atmosphere of the children's case
seminar I had attended in Vienna. So I was doubly
gratified when, following the "Pseudoimbecility" presentation, I could say good-bye to my voluntary position at Mount Sinai and accept a new voluntary
position at the children's service of the New York Psychiatric Institute.

One valuable legacy of my otherwise unsatisfactory
experience at Mount Sinai was my work with a young
patient with multiple tics, really a case of the so-called
Gilles de la Tourette syndrome. I treated this child in
collaboration with Leo Stone, who was extremely
knowledgeable about the neurological aspects of the
child's impairment. At the time I became chief consultant of the children's service of the Psychiatric Institute, I requested, and was granted, the transfer of this
case. The patient in question, whose pseudonym was
Teddy, was subsequently described by Leo Rangell and
me in a paper appearing in the *Psychiatric Quarterly* in
1943[4]; Rangell contributed the neurological part of the
discussion whereas I commented on the psychody-
namic aspects of the case.

On arriving at the Psychiatric Institute in 1941, I
was first greeted by Dr. Irville McKinnon, who informed me of "the rules of the game." The main
thing, he admonished me, was not to get the institution in any trouble. I recall his directive clearly: "If you
have a hot potato, drop it!" By that, he meant that
if a child proved troublesome, he should be dropped,

regardless of how interesting his difficulties were. Apart from this proviso, I was free to proceed with my work as I saw fit.

At the time I began my work at the institute, I also made the acquaintance of Dr. Nolan D. C. Lewis, then Professor and Chairman of the Psychiatry Department at Columbia University. Dr. Lewis was a supportive figure who helped me in my work by coining a pregnant expression—which I no longer recall—to characterize the infant's very early extrauterine experience as lying between constitution and experience.[5] I recall being overwhelmed by his office, the most beautiful I had ever, or have ever since, seen. It had a marvelous view with windows everywhere and was very beautifully furnished.

My own modest office was a different affair. It was underground, and I was very slighted when I discovered that a psychiatric resident, Sam Ritvo, had been assigned the same office without my permission. In retrospect, it was reasonable that the institute should have elected to have me share the office; after all, I was only at the institute one or two days a week whereas Ritvo was full-time. I recall an amusing anecdote apropos this situation. I was very angry at Ritvo's presence and made no bones about expressing it. He went home and told his wife, Lucille, that I had been very curt with him, to which she replied, "Thank goodness. She must like you. Otherwise she would not have said anything." And sure enough, I liked Sam Ritvo, however angry I was at the time at being slighted.

It was owing to the supportive interest of Dr. Lewis

that Dr. Jean Luke and I began our research into child-hood tic disorders. Specifically, Dr. Lewis made available to us, for any project of our choosing, some research money from the Masonic Scottish Rights Fund that the grant recipient, Dr. Reginald Lurie, then in the armed services, had been unable to use. The tic studies, which took the very thoroughly and longitudinally studied case of "Teddy" as a point of departure, eventuated in a series of papers by me and several co-workers. Dr. Luke's and my follow-up study of all the children admitted to the New York State Psychiatric Institute with a diagnosis of "tic" over a ten-to-fifteen-year period led to our important finding, contained in a paper on "Outcome of the Tic Syndrome" (1946),[6] that some of these tiqueurs, whether or not they retained their tic symptoms in later life, became psychotic at puberty.

It was this latter finding, in turn, that stimulated my interest in the relationship between motility—which Freud singled out as one of the ego's principal executive functions—and ego functioning in general. My thinking on this issue led me to understand the steady bombardment of the ego by the tic paroxysms in terms of a weakening of the ego. The ego was simply unable to master these tics, which therefore achieved involuntary discharge through motility. It was this weakened ego that proved unable to cope satisfactorily with the new and stressful tasks brought on by puberty. Finally, it was on the basis of this sequel to my extensive work with the marvelous "tic" population encountered at the Psychiatric Institute that I renewed my interest in childhood psychoses, a topic I first explored at the Institute with Dr. John Ross and Dr. Zaira De Fries.*

This preliminary work on childhood psychosis culminated in a paper exploring and comparing the symptomatology of psychotic children presented at the annual meeting of the American Orthopsychiatric Association in 1948. Entitled "Clinical Studies in Benign and Malignant Cases of Childhood Psychosis (Schizophrenia-like),"[7] it was a very concentrated and careful study that drew on my extensive case material at the Psychiatric Institute. I was astonished at the meeting to discover that my discussant was none other than Leo Kanner, the preeminent authority on "early infantile autism." I am still amused as I recollect the circumstances in which I learned of Kanner's participation in the panel, the names of panel discussants not then being announced beforehand. On my arrival at the meeting, Dr. William Langford greeted me in the lobby and said, "Margaret, I hear that you have written a classic paper." When my only response was "Oh??" he added, "You know who your discussant is? Kanner, and Kanner himself told me that [the paper is a classic]." I believe I would have abandoned the psychosis research at the time of this early communica-

---

*I had already been interested in childhood psychosis in Vienna, where I had two psychotic children in therapy. I was quite certain that these two children were psychotic, which is to say they were neither neurotic, organically impaired, nor amentia cases. I was influenced in my understanding of their pathology by my Rorschach teacher Behn-Eschenburg, who was part of the vanguard of Swiss researchers exploring psychotic disturbance and circumscribing the diagnosis of schizophrenia.

tion if it had not been for the real interest that this very tentative paper awakened in so eminent a colleague as Kanner. He was most encouraging to me at the meeting, pronouncing the paper the first attempt to understand the symptomatology of childhood psychosis dynamically. His only warning was that I should look more carefully at the parents of these children.

It should be remembered that, at this time, in the mid 1940s, there was widespread resistance in both Europe and the United States to the notion that young children could develop pathology that was anything like psychosis—and this despite Kanner's research into "early infantile autism" and Lauretta Bender's trailbreaking work. The resistance was largely emotional; people simply did not want to believe that young children, or even school-age children, could evince disturbances of the magnitude of psychosis. It was in this context, and in the knowledge of this type of resistance, that I began adumbrating my thoughts about childhood psychoses from a dynamic psychoanalytic point of view. And it was in this context that Leo Kanner's enthusiastic reaction to my presentation of 1948 meant so much to me.

These blossoming research interests went hand in hand with the clinical satisfactions afforded by my new position at the Psychiatric Institute. Beginning in 1941, I greatly enjoyed working with the young patients, who took to me like ducks to water. Whenever I worked with a child, that child concentrated all his or her attention on me, regardless of whether or not others were present. The child felt we shared a very special bond—I hesitate to call it "symbiotic," which would be to adopt the prevalent, mistaken use of this term.

Except on those occasional instances in which the child was very, very disturbed, our bond would preserve the integrity and intensity of our dyadic interaction, and I could work with the patient regardless of the number of observers present. Thus it was that, applying techniques to make children feel completely at ease absorbed by osmosis from my teacher Aichhorn, I stunned the Psychiatric Institute community (and colleagues outside this community as well) by presenting child patients before large classes. The children, under these circumstances, felt that the others present did not really count. Their immediate rapport with me overshadowed any other presence to the point that they did not really feel exposed to an audience; they were oblivious to anyone but me. Nonetheless, others did not share my perspective. It was at this time that Marion Kenworthy told her social work students at the New York School of Social Work about this refugee child psychiatrist up at the Psychiatric Institute who made these poor children answer questions before an entire audience, putting them on display, as it were. Later on, she apparently had a change of heart, because she became a good friend, even giving money to help support the therapeutic nursery school at the Masters School that I subsequently founded.

* * *

My various professional activities quickly became so absorbing and time-consuming that my recollections of my personal life in the years immediately following the emigration are necessarily sparse. Shortly after arriving in America, I arranged for the emigration of my childhood friend from Sopron, Vera Farkas Hart, along with her aunt. Vera's parents had been close friends of my parents (her father was a ranking military doctor), and we spent many a summer together in Sopron. On arriving in the United States, Vera entered our household as a housekeeper and immediately imparted a much-needed sense of order to our daily lives. I was, and remained, a very untalented hausfrau, owing in no small measure to my mother's lifelong insistence that I was no good in the house and dire predictions of how I would suffer on account of it. Vera helped me immensely in my everyday life, and I remain grateful for her support and friendship during the difficult transitional years that followed my arrival.

Of course, I remained preoccupied with the fate of my family members throughout the war years. My sister, Suzanne, committed to her musical studies, steadfastly refused to leave Vienna at the time of the Anschluss. Eventually, having suffered greatly, she went clandestinely to Budapest, where she was taken into the family of her very good friends, Professor and Mrs. Tokacs. It was owing to the goodness of these people, who swore to the authorities that Suzanne was a sister of Mrs. Tokacs, that she managed to escape persecution. She returned to Vienna after the war and resumed her musical career.

My parents' sage is infinitely sadder. At the time of the Anschluss, my mother wanted badly to follow Paul and me to America, but nothing came of it. My father died a month before the German invasion of Hungary in 1944. At the time of his death, my mother received urgent messages from the mayor (*Bürgermeister*) of Sopron, urging her to take my father's nurse and cross the border. But my mother refused to grasp the severity of her plight. She had always been an obedient citizen, and she could not then believe that any harm would come to her. She would perish in Auschwitz a year later.

It is a profound and painful irony that my parents' fate might have been very different. My father, it will be recalled, was not only the leading public health officer of Sopron, the recipient of many governmental honors; he was also an influential member of the Hungarian Jewish "elite," the president of the Sopron Jewish community and the guiding spirit and financial sponsor of the town's beautiful home for the Jewish elderly. It was thus that, long before my father's death, both parents were invited, and sent the necessary immigration visas, to resettle in Palestine. But, tragically, the invitation and the visas never found their way to my parents. After the war, my sister located these documents in Budapest; they had never been delivered to our village.[8]

Despite the professional support I received and the friendship and help of Vera Hart, I recall the early and mid forties as a prolonged nightmare owing to the uncertain fate of my sister and parents. Through an American GI with whom I made contact, I was able regularly to send all manner of things, including lightweight clothing, to my sister, toward whom I nonetheless felt considerable ambivalence owing to her apparent failure to take any steps to rescue our mother. My sister and I had no direct contact during the war years, although we got back in touch much later. At the outset of the war, I was occasionally able to hear something about my parents, albeit fourth-hand. Mrs. Merta Bloss was in touch with relatives in Sweden who in turn were in contact with her own parents in Hungary, and her parents would very occasionally hear something about my parents, which would ultimately be relayed back to me.

I quickly realized in the early forties that I could not bear the stifling city environment of New York week-in, week-out. I required a country retreat to which I could periodically escape, at least on those weekends when my schedule permitted. I recall being taken aback by the implicit segregation that I encountered when I began to explore the possibility of obtaining a second residence. Here, a Jew could only buy a summer home in a nonrestricted area. My husband and I had never before encountered this notion of "restriction"; I had been a member of that elite stratum of Hungarian Jewry that had been very much accepted in the Gentile world.

Undaunted by this unsavory aspect of American social life, I set about looking for a summer home along with our friends, Esther and William Menaker, who also wanted a summer home. As it turned out, the Menakers were the first to make a move. They saw an advertisement for an attractive "study" in Brookfield,

Connecticut, and proceeded to rent it. They graciously made this cottage available to Paul and me, albeit with the expectation that I would provide transportation to and from Brookfield. Of the four of us, I alone had a car and was a seasoned driver to boot. For a time, the Menakers and Mahlers planned to buy a summer home together, and even though this plan never materialized, I spent many a weekend seriously looking for a place for the four of us. Finally, when I was at the point of giving up entirely on finding a summer home, I came upon a lovely red house with gingerbread decoration that would be adequate for Paul and me. The house, along with the half-acre lot it came on, was available at the then grand sum of $5,000; I could just barely afford it. So in 1944 I bought my summer home in Brookfield.

Although the Brookfield home was a modest cottage, my decision to go ahead with the purchase occasioned some initial resentment on the part of my husband, since I made the decision on my own and bought the cottage with my own money. Paul was simply not a nature lover, a country person, like me. He was Viennese in every sense of the world. By the time we married in 1936, we had both pretty much settled into our respective professional routines. We shared a common love of music—he insisted on attending live concerts, having a great intolerance for the "canned music" of records—but otherwise had dissimilar hobbies and interests. He was an excellent, in fact a prize-winning bridge player, for example, whereas I had no interest whatsoever in card games. On the other hand,

I greatly enjoyed gardening around the Brookfield cottage, an interest he never shared. In any event, during the summer of 1944 Paul's demanding job in the city made it difficult for him to come to Brookfield very often, so that I came to the summer cottage alone for many weeks of that first summer.

A year after I bought my Brookfield home, in the summer of 1945, I received the news that my mother had been deported and murdered in Auschwitz by the Nazis. It was my great friend Beni Ferenczy, the sculptor, who gently informed me of my mother's fate in a wonderfully touching letter. As I think back to my private life during the years following my arrival in the United States, I think primarily of the long and painful mourning process that followed the news of my mother's death. I was beside myself on learning the news; I had remained terribly involved with my mother even as I understood—and perhaps *because* I understood— that I had been so badly treated by her as a young child. Following the news of her death, I became deeply depressed and spent days on end simply driving my car around the scenic countryside of Brookfield. The only person to whom I unburdened myself was Edith Jacobson, who had purchased a summer home on Long Island shortly after I had purchased our home in Brookfield.

Edith Jacobson became very important to me around this time. I recall extensive discussions with her at the time she began work on her important book, *The Self and the Object World* (1964). At the beginning of our discussions, I had no understanding at all of the concept of representation, being an "experimental animal," so to speak. She taught me the meaning of this concept, and I came to admire her a great deal in the process. When I experienced certain conflicts over my place in the new world of American psychoanalysis, I entered analysis with her and, in one key respect, Edith Jacobson had greater success with me than my Vienna analyst Willi Hoffer: she helped me work through, and ultimately relinquish, a certain tendency to form paranoid ideas. During our analytic work, I did discover, to my surprise, that Edith Jacobson was very intolerant of aggression—surprising in view of her stature as an authority on depression. She was in fact rather punitive about expressions of aggression, and it is probably not coincidental that she unsuccessfully tried to induce a number of her patients, three of whom I knew, to submit to electroshock treatment.

* * *

As I look back on my first decade in America, the pain of private loss is tempered by the joy of emerging professional fulfillment. In Vienna, I had toiled for a decade and a half under the shadow of titans. Awed by Anna Freud, for a time by Helene Deutsch, and by the Vienna Psychoanalytic Institute in general, I reached an impasse, unable to find a voice to express the developmental and clinical insights toward which I was then groping. From about 1925 to 1938 I felt creatively stifled, and this feeling is no doubt reflected in the striking meagerness of my published output during this same period. From 1929, when I published my last preanalytic contribution to the pediatric literature,[9] to 1941, when I made my first forays in the American psychiatric literature,[10] my publication record has but a single entry: my major study of 1938, coauthored with Judith Silberpfennig (later Judith Kestenberg), on the relevance of Rorschach interpretation to understanding the psychology of brain-damaged adults.[11] It was only the stressful situation of emigration and relocation in America that mobilized my creativity, prompting me to bring out of hibernation ideas that had long been slumbering, to communicate them orally, to write them down. For me, then, the stress of emigration, however genuine, however unsettling, was simultaneously the harbinger of a wholesome "new beginning" (Michael Balint); it signifed the falling away of the stamp of eternal student status that the awesome Vienna Psychoanalytic Institute, however unwittingly, bestowed on young analysts. Separation from the Vienna Psychoanalytic Institute was painful, to be sure, but it was also liberating and even exhilarating.

But let me be clear on what it was about this separation that was liberating. It was not simply owing to the stressful circumstances attending the emigration that I became newly creative. It was rather that with the stress came new vistas, new curiosity, new opportunities, and vital new sources of collegial support. It was only in America, and only owing to the tremendous professional encouragement I received in America, that I no longer felt I was laboring under the shadow of titans. If I had not come to America, where I felt free to formulate tentatively insights at which I had empathically arrived, I would have accomplished very little. I would never have begun to publish, to teach, to undertake research. Because if one does not find an assenting echo to one's ideas, if one is passed over, as I was in Vienna, then one cannot create. To create, after all, is to believe that what one says will count.

7 · *Professional Fulfillment*

It was around 1950 that the analytic contingent at the New York Psychiatric Institute was invaded by Sandor Rado and his group. It was brought to my attention that many residents and interns went to Nolan Lewis and appealed to him, prophylactically as it were, to safeguard my status. I stayed on for a while, but as I became increasingly uncomfortable with the growing influence of the Rado group, I resolved to look for another affiliation.

Through 1949, my psychoanalytic work broadly fell into two categories. One category encompassed my studies of tic, including symptomatic tic and tic syndrome, in childhood psychopathology.* The other category encompassed research into childhood psychosis, of which my presentation before the American Orthopsychiatric Association in 1948 was an important signpost. Nineteen fifty was an opportune time not only to change affiliation but to make such a change the occasion for concentrating on the second of these two research tracks. The tic research that had occupied me during the 1940s was at an end, and the two residents who had assisted me with this work, Dr. Jean Luke and Dr. Wilburta Daltroff, had completed their training programs at the Psychiatric Institute. It was in this context that I learned with interest about the newly launched Albert Einstein College of Medicine.

---

*My culminating study in this area was "A Psychoanalytic Evaluation of the Tic in Psychopathology of Children: Symptomatic Tic and Tic Syndrome," *The Psychoanalytic Study of the Child*, 3/4: 279–310, 1949. [Reprinted in *The Selected Papers of Margaret S. Mahler*, vol. I, pp. 37–73 —ed.]

When, on one of his visits to New York, Dr. Milton Rosenbaum visited me and formally invited me to join the Einstein faculty, I was pleased to accept.

I went out to Einstein even before Rosenbaum himself had relocated from Cincinnati to New York, and at a time when Einstein's Jacobi Hospital, though completed, still had no patients. Since Einstein's program was not yet established, the precise nature of my responsibilities evolved over the course of several months on a somewhat ad hoc basis. Joseph Kramer, the head of the child psychiatry department, informed me that I was again to serve as the main consultant to the children's service; I was also asked to hold conferences in child psychiatry. When the hospital was in full swing, I spent some time on the wards, seeing certain children and discussing particular problems with the very efficient head nurse. I also gave a formal children's conference one Thursday each month.

Nineteen fifty also saw the expansion of my teaching activities to Philadelphia, where I was offered and accepted the chairmanship of the child analysis training program of one branch of the recently split Philadelphia Psychoanalytic Institute. I carefully considered the offer, which came from LeRoy M. A. Maeder, as it not only constituted a major pedagogical responsibility, but imposed the hardship of traveling to Philadelphia regularly. I accepted it partly because I am a passionate teacher but also out of frustration with the situation in New York, where conflicts and quarrels about the child analysis chairmanship continued to plague the New York Psychoanalytic Institute. In 1950, the New

York chairmanship undoubtedly belonged to Bertha Bornstein, a first-rate person with whom everyone— and especially I—had trouble getting along.

By the fall of 1950, then, I was commuting to Philadelphia every other weekend and staying there from Friday afternoon until Sunday night or Monday morning. On Friday evenings, I conducted a class on child analysis, and on Saturday mornings I conducted supervisory hours with individual candidates and, later on, an advanced seminar, as well. These efforts notwithstanding, the Philadelphia Institute was in dire need of additional teaching staff. In response to this situation, I instituted, several years after assuming the chairmanship, a regular supervisory seminar in which senior candidates at the institute supervised beginning candidates. The procedure worked as follows: a beginning child analysis candidate's first case would be supervised directly by me, but his or her second case would be supervised by a senior candidate, who was, in turn, supervised by me. At the beginning of the program, the latter supervisory responsibilities fell particularly on Selma Kramer and Calvin Settlage. Some time later, this pedagogical system was adopted by the entire American Psychoanalytic Association, where it became known as "piggyback" supervision.

I commuted to Philadelphia to work with the child analysis candidates throughout the fifties. I continued with this gratifying work into the sixties, though by this time, in recognition of the demands of my schedule, the candidates traveled to New York to see me, rather than the other way around. Most of the candidates trained under my Philadelphia chairmanship graduated from the child analysis program; the original candidates, who now practice throughout the country, include such distinguished child analysts as James Delano, Stewart Finch, Saul Harris, Calvin Settlage, and Selma Kramer.

The Philadelphia Psychoanalytic Institute, and especially its child analysis group, is unabashedly one of my pride and joys. I believe I had much to do with the training, under its auspices, of many of the finest child analysts of the present generation. Of course, there is no denying that many of these individuals were so-called naturals. But it might still be suggested that with a less prodding and less facilitating psychoanalytic teacher-mother, they would have developed neither so quickly nor so well.

While my teaching activities found an important outlet in the Philadelphia Institute in 1950, my research activities remained firmly ensconced in New York. It was at this time, and in the light of my continuing interest in childhood psychosis, that Manuel Furer and I founded a therapeutic nursery for psychotic children at Einstein. I had earlier made Furer's acquaintance as one of his interviewers for admission to the New York Psychoanalytic Institute. He became affiliated with Einstein shortly after I did; our productive collaboration of many years bears witness to the fact that our minds worked much the same way. The therapeutic nursery that we founded at Einstein was intended to continue the work on childhood psychosis I had begun at the New York State Psychiatric Institute.

Furer and I learned much about the management of childhood psychosis from this nursery setting, and our experience was summarized in our joint presentation before the Child Psychiatry Section of the first Pan American Medical Congress, held in Mexico City in May 1960; the paper was published that same year in the *Psychoanalytic Quarterly*.[1]

I should note in passing that whereas this paper of 1960 marked the first systematic description of a symbiotic relationship, the notion of the symbiotic nature of human existence was already spelled out in a footnote to the paper on benign and malignant cases of childhood psychosis published with Ross and De Fries in 1949. There I had maintained that a particular type of childhood psychosis appears to originate in the second half of the first year and the second year of life, whereas another type originates somewhat later. At the time of this paper, I had already arrived at the idea that psychological birth is not simultaneous with biological birth, and this idea, I must again stress, was rooted in my pediatric experience in Vienna. As the head of a large well-baby clinic in the early thirties, I had the feeling that the normal babies brought to us by their mothers were really in a twilight state of existence, unaware of any separate existence outside the symbiotic orbit that "belonged" to their own selves.

But the intellectual ancestry of my notion of "symbiotic syndrome" notwithstanding, it was only in 1955 that Furer and I, convinced that our therapeutic nursery project was pointing toward some major insights about important developmental issues, decided to apply for funding to the National Institute of Mental Health to study the natural history of symbiotic childhood psychosis. The NIMH, at this point in time, was rather sympathetic to analytic work, and especially to analytically inspired research that addressed developmental issues. Dr. Morton Reiser not only directed me to the NIMH as a source of funding but helped me immensely with the task of completing the grant application. I knew full well that I would not be able to answer questions such as "What do you expect to find and with what methods?" In fact, it was the contemplation of just such questions that delayed my applications for research grants for a good ten years! If I knew what I would find, let alone what methods I would employ to find what I would find—so I thought—I would not be interested in undertaking the research in the first place. This was a rather short-sighted view of what research applications are all about, to say the least!

In any event, with Reiser's assistance, I completed the application and, lo and behold, Furer and I got the grant. To the amazement and chagrin of my colleagues at Einstein, however, we turned around and returned the grant money to NIMH in 1956! What had happened? To make a long story short, as Furer and I continued to ponder a methodology and institutional setup adequate to the questions we were asking, it became clear that Einstein could not support such a research project. The institution was then in its infancy, and the research project we were envisioning would have placed an inordinate burden on both facilities and staff.

At this stage in its existence, Einstein rightly took the teaching of students to be its paramount task, and our research project, in our considered judgment, would have compromised its effectiveness as a fledgling teaching institution. I was further put off by the administrative red tape that would encumber the operation of our nursery in such an academic setting. The mothers who, with their children, would be participating in the project would hardly feel at ease if I had to write out a formal request every time they wanted a glass of tomato juice.

So I announced to Milton Rosenbaum that I wanted to return the grant money to NIMH, explaining that I had no recriminations whatsoever but simply felt that Einstein was, and ought to remain, completely committed to teaching its students. He reacted with outright horror, exclaiming ''Margaret, one does not send back money!'' To which I replied, ''Milt, 'one' won't, but 'I' will!'' Fortunately, Sybil Escalona, who had just arrived at Einstein at the time, understood very well my reasoning and joined me in persuading Rosenbaum to see things our way. The two of us then collaborated on a very frank letter to NIMH in which I explained, as honestly as possible, why I could not undertake the research it had agreed to fund. In declining this generous grant, for which I expressed great thanks nonetheless, I could not help but think that I would never again receive a penny from NIMH, and the status of the therapeutic nursery was of course up in the air.

But very soon afterwards, a very American thing

happened, in the best sense of the word. In 1956, the Masters School, located at 75 Horatio Street, received an unexpected windfall in the form of two lovely buildings in Greenwich Village. The buildings were donated to the school by an alumnus. Both buildings were already equipped to be nursery schools, and the board of directors of the school was at a loss as to what to do with them. It was at this juncture that the board learned from Mrs. Margaret Freed that Dr. Furer and I had a project for a therapeutic nursery that could be very nicely implemented in these two buildings. They approached us, sounded us out, and made us an offer—albeit one that did not entail any significant funding on the part of the school.

The buildings in question were virtually ideal for our purposes. They were isolated from an academic setting and the bureaucratic red tape that such a setting entailed. In these buildings mothers could be mothers in a relatively natural and unmonitored way. So, without further ado, Furer and I immediately accepted the offer and relocated the Einstein therapeutic nursery project in the two Greenwich Village buildings, which we dubbed the Masters Children's Center.

The lack of funding proved troublesome. Although the board members of the Masters School welcomed our use of the two buildings, they were disinclined to spend any money—certainly not the money of alumni or Board members!—to fund the day-to-day operation of the center. Fortunately, several influential board members, including Mary J. Crowther, then a member of the editorial staff of the *Psychoanalytic Quarterly,* and

Jessen Stanton, prominent in nursery school circles, rose to our defense. They were appalled by the pettiness of most of the members toward our worthwhile project. And so it was that, from 1957 to 1959, the generous moral support of the board was supplemented by heavy financial support.

In fact, the Masters School's somewhat grudging support notwithstanding, the Masters Children's Center had to struggle to keep afloat financially during its early years, and I doubt Furer and I would have lasted very long at this location had we not been encouraged to reapply to NIMH for the same funding it had formerly made available for Einstein-based research. We did so in 1959 and, to our great surprise—given the fact that we were now affiliated with an institution wholly unknown to NIMH officialdom—we received the very five-year grant we had earlier declined. Of course, this time around we know perfectly well that we wanted to investigate the naural history of symbiotic childhood psychosis, and the strength of my name in this area probably went far in inducing NIMH to give us the money.* At any rate, this grant provided the much-needed financial base for a study that yielded a score of papers and, eventually, my book of 1968, *On Human Symbiosis and the Vicissitudes of Individuation: Infantile Psychosis.*

---

*I later learned from a member of the NIMH enclave that, at the time of Furer's and my second application, it had been remarked in the relevant committee "that if Margaret Mahler finds it expedient to get up from her easy chair to do this research, then we really should help her."

At the time the therapeutic nursery established at Einstein was transplanted to the Masters Children's Center, it counted as its enrollees four or five very disturbed children and one child who was genuinely psychotic. It was immediately apparent that one of the two nursery teachers had to be entirely at the disposal of the single psychotic child. This observation reinforced Furer's and my verdict, which we had already reached at Einstein, that one simply cannot undertake meaningful therapeutic work with, much less hope to rehabilitate, psychotic children without a one-to-one relationship. Once at the Masters Children's Center, we incorporated this insight into our research methodology via the so-called tripartite design for the therapy of psychotic children.

The tripartite design implicated the mother in her child's therapy; she was to be present during at least the first part of the child's one-to-one treatment by a child therapist. At the same time, the mother herself was assigned a social worker for supplementary counseling. This entire process was overseen and supervised by one of the senior child psychiatrists (i.e., Dr. Furer or me). In the course of supervising the work of the child therapists, Dr. Furer and I would, even after the first phase of treatment, ask mothers to come and observe their children in interaction with the children's therapists. This proved an effective way of making the mother feel part of the treatment process. It was our expectation that, through identification with the child's therapist over the course of the tripartitely designed therapy, the mother would become the *kind* of mother with whom the psychotic child could now experience the relatively normal symbiotic relationship he or she had never had in early life. On the basis of this symbiotic relationship, in turn, the child would gradually acquire the capacity to separate and individuate intrapsychically, that is, to experience himself, metaphorically speaking, as separate and as an individual.

Very soon after we had implemented this tripartite treatment design at the Masters Children's Center, I asked myself the following question: why is it that the vast majority of infants *do* emerge with a firm sense of their own entity and identity by three years of age, whereas those infants who do *not* (i.e., those prepsychotic babies in our therapeutic nursery) represent so minuscule a percentage of all infants? The outcome of these musings was a pilot study with average mothers and their normal babies, headed by Dr. Furer.[2] Furer and I believed it would be most instructive to compare the interaction between the mothers and seriously disturbed children in the "psychosis study" with a control group of normal mothers with normal babies (i.e., babies proceeding normally in their ego development and identity formation). Aided by a small grant from the Field Foundation, we recruited our first control group by word of mouth, being fortunate in having a neighborhood nursery school proximate to the Masters Center. We invited neighborhood mothers to bring us their younger babies—initially nine months and older—advising them that we were interested in investigating the development of normal children.

We were prepared to offer the local mothers certain

enticements to induce them to participate in our pilot study, but as it turned out, such enticements were totally unnecessary. It is not hard to surmise why our initial invitation elicited so positive a response. We offered the mothers and their infants a beautiful naturalistic setting, an indoor playground in which the infants could romp and the mothers could socialize. For the young mothers, frequently lonely, this latter function was especially important: we offered them the companionship of other young mothers in the same boat, which is to say, we offered them membership in a veritable "mothers club" of young mothers. These women found the naturalistic character of study participation equally to their liking. Once inside the Masters Center, they had complete autonomy to be mothers, i.e., to interact with and monitor their children as they saw fit. They were not obliged even to acknowledge the presence of the staff. At the same time, they certainly liked the idea that sympathetic professionals were available for help should problems develop.

* * *

Since it was at this point in my career that my research on childhood psychosis began giving pride of place to research on normal development, and especially the separation-individuation process as an integral dimension of that development, it is perhaps appropriate to pause briefly to reflect on these twin preoccupations and the reasons the former ultimately gave way to the latter. My several decades of research and therapy with severely disturbed children had always subtended, without supplanting, my main interest in normal development, and especially the process by which the "average" human being becomes a discrete "entity" with a personal identity. Perhaps because I had witnessed for so long and with such thoroughness how relatively little one can do once a child has actually become psychotic, I reached a point at which I wanted to let my developmental and clinical insights subserve an understanding of normal development. It is the latter type of understanding, with its implications for primary prevention and early intervention, that offers potential benefits to the overwhelming majority of mental health professionals—to many more workers than can benefit from, and utilize findings derived from, the intensive longitudinal treatment of a single child. To be sure, I had done more than my share of intensive, continuing therapy with seriously disturbed children in Europe, and I had learned a great deal from this work. But the import of this experience, once more, was to convince me of just how little one can accomplish with truly psychotic children. I recall one of my European patients, a little boy named Burli, who wrote me completely psychotic letters after many years of treatment.

Despite my great admiration for therapists, like my colleague Anni Bergman, who can work intensively and fruitfully with a single patient for a decade or more, I myself do not have the infinite patience required, and I am not primarily interested in the yield of such long-term immersion in a single patient at any rate. For me, rather, the general problem of identity, and especially the way in which one arrives at a sense of self, has always been primary. Research involving psychosis was, to my mind, always a point of departure for learning about the emerging identity and sense of self of the average child. To make this admission is not to compromise my primary identity as a healer. I am interested in the therapeutic process, perhaps more than Freud and even Anna Freud. In fact, it is out of my identity as a healer that I was led to focus increasingly on issues of normal development, because it is only out of such knowledge that we can formulate those strategies of primary prevention and early intervention that hold out the greatest hope for humankind. But to be a healer with a primary therapeutic mission is not necessarily to be a lifelong advocate of research into the healing process that typifies those very rare and tragically severe cases of what Kanner designated "early infantile autism," and I prefer to characterize as autistic childhood psychosis.

It was in the context of these concerns and priorities that the pilot study comparing seriously disturbed babies and their mothers and normal babies and their mothers at the Masters Children's Center was undertaken in 1962; it marked the beginning of my formal transition from psychosis research to research into normal development. It was via this project that I began to address systematically the major question that has preoccupied me ever since: by what steps does the average infant emerge from the twilight state of symbiosis, separate from the mother, and go on to achieve a sense of entity and identity?

At first, the staff of the psychosis study more or less

assumed responsibility for the complementary "normal" study: Herman Roiphe, Ann Heberle, Manuel Furer, Anni Bergman, and I can be counted the original staff, along with Edith Atkin, our very helpful participant observer, Emmogene Kamaiko, who later headed the "toddler" group in the normal study, and Laura Malkinson, our official photographer. Dr. David Meyer, a child psychiatrist, became a part-time member shortly thereafter; his salary was paid by the National Association for Mental Health, which directed him to compare the development of intelligence in the group of psychotic infants and toddlers with the group of normal infants and toddlers. Via the initial grant from the Field Foundation, Dr. Meyer's grant, and modest supplementary grants from the Grant Foundation and the Taconic Foundation, we carried on with our two complementary projects: the childhood psychosis project upstairs and the "normal" project downstairs. The latter, following my use of the expression, soon became known as the "separation-individuation" project.

I should perhaps comment on how the term *separation-individuation* originated. Back in 1954, Bert Gosliner read to the New York Psychoanalytic Society a paper that he and I coauthored.[3] We described a tiqueur, an adolescent suffering from multiple tics and tic paroxysms who was simultaneously enmeshed in a symbiotic-parasitic relationship with his mother. He would beg his mother to come near but, as soon as she did so, would bodily reject her. Using this case as a pathological exemplar, we proceeded to describe the process by which the normal baby, step by step, established a viable identity and sense of him- or herself as a separate entity. In the discussion that followed Gosliner's reading of the paper, Annemarie Weil asked us why, having described a process that encompassed issues of separation and issues of individuation, we did not characterize the entire process as "separation hyphen individuation." So she is really responsible for the use of the term insofar as she made the recommendation at the time.

At the time of the 1954 presentation and for several years thereafter, we thought that the essential process of separation-individuation took place in the second year of life. On the basis of the original pilot study funded by the Field Foundation, however, my colleagues and I observed that our nine- to twelve-month-old infants were already in rather advanced stages of the process; at the very least, they had already differentiated their body image from that of the mother. Spurred by this early finding, we accepted infants into the program at increasingly early ages. By the third or fourth year of the study, we took infants almost from birth. When these infants reached the age of four or five months, we began studying them and their mothers intensively, via systematic filming and the use of both participant and nonparticipant observers, according to the methodology described in the appendix to *The Psychological Birth of the Human Infant* (1975).

It is not my intention here to expound at length on this methodology, but let me at least highlight its salient features and comment briefly on the observational yield of our approach. It should be pointed out, first of all, that our study design was cross-sectional in nature. By this, I mean that we were less interested in observing the differences between children of different ages than in comparing children of the same age. Via this methodology, of course, infants and toddlers could not only be compared with one another at a given age but subsequently compared with *themselves* over time. In fact, it was by comparing infants and toddlers of a particular age over time that we were able to observe those characteristics that typify particular age periods. Our description of these characteristics amounted to a kind of choreography of the interchange between mother and baby. It encompassed the baby's gestures, the mother's responses, the mother's mirroring of the baby, and so on, and it explored these aspects of the mother-baby interchange all the way down to the minute particulars of their behavior at the Center: the way the mother brought her child to the Center; removed his wraps; put him down; whether or not, on arriving, she left the child alone; and so on. All these constituents of what Spitz taught us to recognize as the "dialogue" between mother and child yielded important insights into general patterns that repeat themselves over time in all reasonably normal children. Derivatively, of course our observation and description of this dialogue did alert us to the differences between two babies of the same age, even newborns. If a particular baby did not evince the general age-appropriate patterns that fell within a particular developmental line, we analyzed this difference, this unevenness.

Out of this methodology, two main tracks of development could be discerned, one serving *individuation* and the other serving intrapsychic *separation* from the mothering one. Individuation coincides with the evolution of ego functions such as perception, memory, and reality testing. Separation, on the other hand, is the intrapsychic achievement of differentiation from the mother, with the boundary formation that attends such differentiation; it is served mainly by the motor apparatus in the form of the child's motility.

Of course, the tracks of individuation and separation, while optimally proceeding hand in hand, are not always synchronous. From the beginning, for example, we observed certain children who were early walkers but did not realize they were separate from their mothers. In such children, cognitive functioning had not kept pace with the precocious functioning of the motor apparatus. Via their motor ability, they could wander much farther from the maternal "home base" than was either comfortable or safe. As we watched them motorically explore their environment, we witnessed interludes of sudden perplexity and bewilderment; it was as if such children would suddenly stop and say, "Where am I? Where is my symbiotic part?" Significantly, those children who were relatively late walkers seemed more advanced in their cognitive functioning (perception, memory, reality testing) at particular junctures of development than the early walkers.

On the basis of the "normal" pilot study employing this methodology, I was able to postulate four regularly occurring steps in the separation-individuation process, steps that anyone can verify who replicates the study. The first subphase of the separation-individuation process, which overlaps with a period I termed "after symbiosis," is the *differentiation* subphase. At the time the pilot study was taking place at the Masters Children's Center, we characterized this subphase as the infant's "hatching" from the mother-infant symbiotic orbit. When the toddler alights and walks away from the mother (not *toward* the mother; the toddler's first steps are usually *away* from the mother), we say that he or she has entered the second subphase of the separation-individuation process, the *practicing* subphase. Between sixteen and twenty-four months and beyond, the toddler experiences the crucially important *rapprochement* subphase; and, finally, from about two to three years of age and beyond, the toddler enters an open-ended stage that I like to call "on the way to emotional object constancy."

In 1963, I decided that I had had enough of the psychosis study and wanted to devote all my time to the "normal" study. It was at this time that I therefore asked Dr. Furer to take over the psychosis project completely, while I applied for, and received, NIMH funding for a four- to five-year project dealing with the normal separation-individuation process. The following year, Dr. John McDevitt approached me about participating in the "normal" research. I had met McDevitt in 1952, when I had supervised his analytic treatment of his second adult patient. Even at that early date, I had been struck by his focal interest in severe deviations in the development of object constancy. He came to me in the summer of 1964 from the Yale Child Study Center, where he had participated in a longitudinal study similar to mine headed by Ernst Kris. He had been viewing my research appreciatively from afar, so to speak. I was tickled pink when he compared me especially with Kris, the most congenial and wonderful teacher I have ever known. He began working with me in January 1965 and became my closest associate.

Earlier still, in 1958, I met Dr. Fred Pine at a therapeutic nursery run by the Hudson Guild Settlement on the Lower West Side. I gave several hours a week as a consultant to the nursery, whereas Pine was performing psychological assessments of the nursery children. Shortly thereafter, in 1960, I invited Pine to join the "normal" staff as chief psychologist. With his arrival on the staff, followed by that of McDevitt several years later, the principals of the research team whose findings would eventuate in *The Psychological Birth of the Human Infant* were assembled.

Epilogue · Thoughts on Separation-Individuation

One of my earliest memories—a screen memory, no doubt—concerns a surreptitious, naughty act committed as a four or five year old. Rumor had it that a neighbor's cat, housed with her new litter in the attic of our apartment building, was whelping. Propelled by unusual curiosity, with an eagerness to get to the source of the whelping, I clandestinely snuck up to the attic. I recall being appalled at the condition of the newborn kittens, which, owing to their sealed eyelids, could not see. I promptly set about righting this situation, that is, I began prying apart their eyelids. In the manner of children, I was unaware of the danger to my own eyes presented by the mother cat, which might have instinctively attacked me in defense of her young.

I believed that the germ of two of my major articles, "Pseudoimbecility: A Magic Cap of Invisibility" (1942) and "Les Enfants Terribles" (1949),[1] lay hidden in this episode. But perhaps more importantly still, I believe the same curiosity that impelled me to explore the status of these newborn kittens in their maternal surround spurred me to raise a different, albeit related, question some thirty-five years later: why is it that symbiotic and autistic children cannot distinguish between themselves and their mothers and, more broadly, between themselves and others? Either they have erected a wall to ward off the mother, who is thereby imperceptible to them as a living being, or they have failed to create a boundary between themselves and the mother in the first place. But given the plight of these children, why is it that the overwhelming majority of human beings do, in short order, arrive at a discrete, albeit primitive, sense of themselves as separate entities with individual identities?

The conceptualization and description of the separation-individuation process are of course the outcome of over a quarter century of research aimed at illuminating these profound, and profoundly important, questions. This research has shown how the child's attainment of his complementary senses of entity and identity is the product of a gradual separation and individuation out of the primary matrix of the mother-infant relationship. From the standpoint of separation-individuation theory, this process is equated with the child's psychological birth.

Although it is a source of gratification to me that this theory has enjoyed widespread acceptance among analysts, child psychiatrists, and other mental health workers, it is a source of frustration that this theory, like all theories, has given rise to misunderstanding, even among those who endorse it. The tendency to construe failures in the separation-individuation process as instances of "ego distortion" or "ego disturbance," for example, remains widespread. To impute ego distortion or ego disturbance to the child is, to most clinicians and researchers, to imply a developmental arrest or lag. But to conceptualize this arrest or lag in terms of the separation-individuation process is to go beyond general developmental considerations, and to assign both a specificity and a complexity to the "distortion" or "disturbance" in question. It is to say, for example, that the developmental arrest at issue is understandable as the sequel to an unresolved rapprochement subphase. To invoke the rapprochement subphase, in turn, is to implicate a very complex developmental arrest that may encompass several aspects of the personality: those dealing with the body image, with object relationships, with separation anxiety, with the need for narcissistic supplies, and so on. It is the range of complex issues devolving on a particular subphase of the separation-individuation process that is routinely ignored by those who are content to speak etiologically of ego distortion or ego disturbance. To grasp fully the implications of the separation-individuation process is, in fact, to emerge with a thoroughgoing revision of the very concept of infantile neurosis, a revision that is incompatible with the global label of ego distortion or ego disturbance.*

It is not without reason that I chose, by way of illustrating my viewpoint, those conflicts pertaining to the rapprochement subphase of the separation-individuation process. Most children who enter analysis these days have failed to resolve the rapprochement crisis that my coworkers (especially John McDevitt) and I have described repeatedly and minutely. I believe that heightened attentiveness to the significance of the rapprochement subphase accounts, in part, for the increased recognition of the crucial role of preoedipal de-

---

*For my conception of the status of infantile neurosis in the light of the separation-individuation process, see my paper, "On the Current Status of the Infantile Neurosis," *Journal of the American Psychoanalytic Association,* 23:327–33, 1975. [Reprinted in *The Selected Papers of Margaret S. Mahler,* vol. II, 189–93 —ed.]

terminants in both psychopathology and the kind of mental health at which one ultimately arrives.

The Oedipus complex, to be sure, forms the core of both normal development and the "normal" infantile neurosis. But the oedipal constellation itself is shaped by what preceded it, and especially by what preceded it during the rapprochement subphase.* As a child first becomes aware of his status as a separate, helpless, and very small individual—a realization that was impossible six months earlier, when this same child, in the midst of the practicing subphase, appeared to believe that "the world is his oyster"—there comes, whether gradually or suddenly, a concomitant realization that he is very much dependent on his mother, that this mother is separate from him, and that she and the father have their own interests and lives. The toddler realizes, in short, that he is by no means the center of the universe. This is the rapprochement crisis.

Now our extensive investigations have shown that the rapprochement crisis is clearly a ubiquitous phenomenon. It can be very mild and barely perceptible or, alternatively, very noisy and dramatic. One can see it everywhere—on the street, in the subway, and in the

---

*Having made this point for the record, I should quickly add that I am much less "preoedipal" in my clinical orientation than many of my pupils. Our diagnostic ability to identify the various subphase issues and conflicts that shape the Oedipus complex is not tantamount to our clinical ability to "undo" serious structural deficiencies rooted in these preoedipal subphases. The import of my developmental theory notwithstanding, I remain a rather orthodox analyst.

supermarket, where it gains expression as the overt struggle between the small child and his mother. If all goes well, the child gradually realizes that he is only a child and that his mother can be cross while still remaining "good." In tandem with this realization, an entire gamut of affects are gradually reconciled and integrated.

Although a measure of rapprochement crisis is as normal and unavoidable as oedipal conflicts, it is nonetheless incumbent on all mental health workers to see to it that children resolve this crisis as quickly and painlessly as possible. The key concept in respect of this goal is, of course, that of the "mothering one," by which we include not only the status of the mother in the present, but the history of the mother-child relationship that precedes the rapprochement subphase. Accurate knowledge of this developmental landmark should be incorporated into the education of child care workers, pediatricians, psychiatrists, and parents alike. With respect to the latter, we must help mothers, and fathers as well, not to become unduly alarmed when their small children experience this unavoidable crisis. We must help them understand that the rapprochement crisis is a normal occurrence of limited duration with respect to which neither they nor their children are at fault.

I believe it is necessary to reiterate what are by now truisms because we live in a society in which child abuse has become an urgent social problem and in which mothers, in turn, tend to be very much maligned. But it is precisely owing to extensive research into the subphases of the separation-individuation process that we now recognize that it is the "ordinary devoted mother," to use Winnicott's term, who often needs help. This is the mother we need to reassure as to the inevitability, for example, of the rapprochement crisis, with the stress and strain it entails. We must explain to these mothers that their own minds may well be in a state of turmoil during the rapprochement subphase. This is the period of early development when the child may be an angel one moment and a kind of monster the next. The "ordinary devoted mother," under these trying circumstances, may feel that she is being needlessly tormented by a monster of a child she does not deserve or, alternatively, that she is an inadequate mother.

If we can convey a basic scientific understanding of the meaning of the rapprochement crisis to mothers and fathers, we will have taken an important step en route to a strategy of prevention of childhood psychopathology and early intervention in those instances where, the best efforts of parents notwithstanding, such psychopathology nonetheless supervenes. Knowledge of the rapprochement crisis, of course, is merely emblematic of knowledge of the separation-individuation process writ large. We must educate parents as to the pitfalls and landmarks of vulnerability throughout the process. To impart general knowledge of this sort is as important as to undertake further research aimed at refining our understanding of the process. And this is because the education of parents subserves prevention and early intervention, which, to my mind, are the answer to major problems of our time. Dr. Louise Kaplan's recent book, *Oneness and Separateness,*[2] should be mentioned as an important building block toward these twin goals. Kaplan has translated the entire separation-individuation process into a language that is at once poetic and popular, with symbiosis and symbiotic tendencies being equated with "oneness," whereas the separation-individuation process tends toward "separateness." In describing the concepts of the separation-individuation process in an appealing and accessible language that the lay public, and especially mothers and fathers, can read with great pleasure, Kaplan has performed a tremendous education service. I believe that *Oneness and Separateness* may become as helpful to parents of this generation as Benjamin Spock's famous book was to the last one.

At the same time as we make our current understanding of the separation-individuation process subserve the important social goals of prevention and early intervention, we must forge ahead with new research that elaborates this understanding with respect to heretofore unexplored topics. The establishment and vicissitudes of so-called core gender identity are among the important issues that the abundant longitudinal data of separation-individuation studies could illuminate. I believe that such research will bear out a conviction of mine that is not shared by many analysts and nonanalysts, to wit, that separation-individuation as a line of development runs parallel to, and is completely compatible with, Freud's libido theory. I believe, furthermore, that the separation-individuation process can serve as a bridge, integrating libido theory with the understanding of gender identity and gender characteristics embodied in the writings of Eleanor Galenson and Herman Roiphe, and Robert Stoller, among others. Such work would, perforce, place a greater emphasis on the development of sexuality than the original research on the separation-individuation process. Here I allude to one aspect of what is perhaps the next great challenge awaiting the efforts of infant researchers: to explore and demarcate the interrelationship between the two great organizing principles of contemporary psychoanalysis, libido theory on the one hand and the separation-individuation process on the other.

Afterword *by* Paul E. Stepansky

Since a memoir is, by definition, a subjective recounting of episodes from a life, it is necessarily skewed along certain lines. This truism is not a pejorative commentary on the memoirist's intent. Rather, it speaks to the fact that to recount one's life at all is to recount it from a particular perspective at a chosen point in time. To have memoirs, we may say, is to have an agenda for the memoirs.

The story that Margaret Mahler tells concentrates on her professional development, with the trials and tribulations therein recounted being attendant to that development. The following facts pertain to a facet of her life and identity treated only in passing in the memoirs: her relationship to Judaism. I offer them here because they contribute to a more rounded understanding of her personality; they also cast in bold relief her reminiscences about the anti-Semitism encountered over the course of her medical training.[1]

Dr. Mahler's recollections of the anti-Semitism encountered in Munich in 1920, when she and her sister Suzanne were imprisoned for several hours, and in Jena in 1921, where she was the target of attack by the Jena chapter of the German-wide student organization (*Allgemeiner Studenten Ausschuss*), do not fully encompass the trajectory of this dimension of her life. When she was very young, perhaps four years old, she later recalled, she heard about pogroms threatening her paternal grandmother, who lived in Esterhaza, where her father had been born. As a result of these threats, this grandmother came to live with the Mahler family, sharing a room with Margaret herself. Several years later, when Mahler was seven (1904), she experienced anti-Semitism as the only Jewess in the private elementary school in which she was enrolled. She recalled a little circular sent around her class that contained the following sentence: "Don't talk to Schönberger because the Israelites have crucified Jesus Christ."

In the memoirs, Dr. Mahler recounts that her mother, Eugenie Wiener Schönberger, perished in Auschwitz in 1944. It bears noting that other close relatives were also victims of the Holocaust. Her mother's sister Irma, with whom Dr. Mahler stayed during her gymnasium years in Budapest, had a son one year older than Mahler. In the memoirs, Mahler recollects that this cousin, "a very good friend of mine," was killed by the Nazis. Her father's older brother Karl had a daughter, Lilly Mohacsi, who married a Hungarian writer. When the writer was taken by the Nazis during the early months of the occupation of Hungary, Lilly either committed suicide or was killed. Another cousin, Sandor, a lawyer and a Mason, was torn to pieces by dogs in Sopron. And finally, a great niece, together with her husband and two children, committed suicide in Budapest the night before they were scheduled for deportation.

In point of fact, the entire Jewish community of Sopron, Dr. Mahler's native village, was virtually wiped out by the Nazis. At the time of the German occupation of March 1944, the town had 1,856 Jewish residents. Over the course of the next two months, 1,470 of these Jews were deported to concentration camps, 40 were arrested, 286 were conscripted for forced labor, 55 were infirm elderly, and 5 were declared "honorary citizens" and allowed to remain.[2]

These facts lend poignancy to Dr. Mahler's recollection of learning, years after her father's death, that the relief agency HIAS had obtained a special permit for both her parents to emigrate to Palestine, which, sadly, did not reach them in time. Likewise, they add special meaning to her final wishes about the disposition of her and her husband Paul's ashes. Approximately eight years before her death, Dr. Mahler expressed the wish and, through the Joint Distribution Committee, made all the necessary arrangements for, the interment of her ashes and those of her late husband, Dr. Paul H. Mahler, in the Jewish Cemetery in Sopron beside the grave of her father, Dr. Gusztav Schönberger. She arranged, in this same context, to have her mother's name engraved on her father's tombstone, and above her name the words "Martyr of the Holocaust." At the time Dr. Mahler's ashes were buried in the Sopron Jewish cemetary, on August 1, 1986, there were only sixteen Jews living in Sopron, including those who returned after the war and their survivors. It bears noting that Dr. Mahler bequeathed $25,000 to the Jewish community of Sopron with a request for perpetual maintenance of her grave and the grave of her father.

Margaret Mahler's lifelong affirmation of her Jewishness, which coexisted with her nonobservance, gained expression in curious and moving ways. Her friend and lawyer Bernard Fischman recalls that in 1970 he showed Mahler Freud's preface of 1930 to the Hebrew translation of *Totem and Taboo* (1913).[3] In this preface, Freud pronounced himself an author "ignorant of the language of holy writ, who is completely estranged from the religion of his father—as well as from every other religion—and who cannot take a share in nationalist ideals, but who has yet never repudiated his people, who feels that he is in his essential nature a Jew and who has no desire to alter that nature." Freud went on to admit, however, that "If the question were put to him: 'Since you have abandoned all these common characteristics of your countrymen, what is there left to you that is Jewish?' he would reply: 'A very great deal, and probably its very essence.' He [Freud] could not now express that essence clearly in words; but some day, no doubt, it will become accessible to the scientific mind." On seeing Freud's striking avowal of his own Jewishness, Mahler offered Fischman the following spontaneous reminiscence. On arriving in England in 1938 and seeing the British Union Jack, she felt a sense of security she had long lost in Vienna. On arriving in the United States six months later and seeing the Stars and Stripes, she felt a still greater sense of security. But one evening, years later, when she was driving a car in Manhattan and saw a lit synagogue, she felt the greatest sense of security of all. It is perhaps fitting that in 1985, the year of her death, Margaret Mahler attended Rosh Hashanah services at New York's Temple Emanu-El. It was the first time, she told her companion, Peggy Hammond, that she had set foot in a synagogue in almost half a century—the last time being during her brief stay in London in 1938.

Whether as parents, educators, or therapists, we are all beneficiaries of the fruits of Margaret Mahler's lifelong labors. To this extent, we share equally in her wealth. But it is perhaps fitting to conclude this afterword by noting how Margaret Mahler chose to share her monetary assets with posterity since, in this decision, too, she reveals herself to us. Dr. Mahler named as the sole residuary legatee of her estate the Grey Panthers Project Fund with the request that her legacy be used to assist elderly, indigent academicians and scholars in their work.

Notes

Introduction

1. Margaret S. Mahler, Fred Pine, and Anni Bergman, *The Psychological Birth of the Human Infant* (New York: Basic Books, 1975), p. 44. On Mahler's understanding of symbiosis and the "normal symbiotic phase," see "On Human Symbiosis and the Vicissitudes of Individuation" (1967) and "Symbiosis and Individuation: The Psychological Birth of the Human Infant" (1974) in *The Selected Papers of Margaret S. Mahler,* vol. II (New York: Jason Aronson, 1979), pp. 78–79, 154–55. In *Psychological Birth,* the topic is covered on pp. 43–51 and a clear definition is provided in the "glossary of concepts," pp. 290–91.

2. On Mahler's understanding of autism and the "normal autistic phase," see "On Human Symbiosis and the Vicissitudes of Individuation," *Selected Papers,* vol. II, pp. 77–78 and *Psychological Birth,* pp. 41–43, 290.

3. Jay R. Greenberg and Stephen A. Mitchell, *Object Relations in Psychoanalytic Theory* (Cambridge, MA: Harvard University Press, 1983), p. 283.

4. Mahler et al., *Psychological Birth,* p. 23.

5. John Bowlby, *Attachment,* 2nd ed. (New York: Basic Books, 1982), p. 179.

6. Ibid., p. 199.

7. Bowlby himself observes that his usage of the word separation as implying the temporary inaccessibility of the subject's attachment figure "should be distinguished from the very different usage of Mahler (1968) who employs it to describe an intrapsychic process which results in 'differentiation of the self from the symbiotic object.'" See John Bowlby, *Separation* (New York: Basic Books, 1973), p. 23n.

8. Bowlby, *Attachment,* p. 216.

9. Mahler et al., *Psychological Birth,* p. 45. Cf. "On Human Symbiosis and the Vicissitudes of Individuation," *Selected Papers,* vol. II, p. 79: "The rudimentary ego in the newborn baby and the young infant has to be complemented by the emotional rapport of the mother's nursing care, a kind of social symbiosis."

10. Bowlby, *Attachment,* p. 228.

11. Mahler et al., *Psychological Birth,* p. 18.

12. Ibid., pp. 24–25.

13. Mahler's major papers on "infantile psychosis" are collected in her *Selected Papers,* vol. I, Part III.

14. According to Mahler, the "rapprochement" subphase, beginning around the fifteenth month and continuing through at least the end of the second year, is the third subphase of the separation-individuation process. At this time, the toddler has already separated from his mother to the point of experiencing conflict between his fear of losing the mother's love and his fear of being swallowed up or "engulfed" by this same love, thereupon losing his emerging sense of identity. It is the rapprochement struggle, culminating in what Mahler terms the "rapprochement crisis," that frequently shapes those neurotic disturbances that emerge during the somewhat later oedipal period. On the relevance of the rapprochement subphase to neurotic conflict, see "Rapprochement Subphase of the Separation-Individuation Process" (1972) and "On the Current Status of the Infantile Neurosis" (1975) in *Selected Papers,* vol. II, especially pp. 147, 193, and *Psychological Birth,* pp. 225–30.

15. Margaret S. Mahler, *On Human Symbiosis and the Vicissitudes of Individuation* (New York: International Universities Press, 1968), p. 32.

16. Karl Joachim Weintraum, *The Value of the Individual: Self and Circumstance in Autobiography* (Chicago: University of Chicago Press, 1978), chapter 1.

17. Ibid., p. xviii.

18. Around this same time, Dr. Mahler also collaborated with Dr. Darlene Levy in the preparation of a twenty-four page "précis" of her memoirs. This document contains brief two-to-three page summaries of the successive phases of her career.

Dr. Levy's support of Dr. Mahler's resolve to lay the groundwork for memoirs is herewith noted. She not only encouraged Dr. Mahler to proceed with the Nagel interviews but arranged for the preparation of typed transcripts of the interviews.

19. It is perhaps relevant to note that, shortly before my first meeting with Dr. Mahler, Dr. Nagel had given her a copy of my recently published study of Alfred Adler, *In Freud's Shadow: Adler in Context* (Hillsdale, NJ: The Analytic Press, 1983), with its favorable assessment of the psychoanalytic pedagogy of her most important mentor, August Aichhorn (pp. 222ff.). At the time of our first meeting, Dr. Mahler had my book by her side and was most generous in her estimation of it.

Chapter 1 Sopron

1. In *Women in Mathematics* (Cambridge, MA: MIT Press, 1974), L. M. Osen begins her account of Sonja Corvin-Krukovsky Kovalevsky (1850–1891) by proclaiming her "perhaps the most dazzling mathematical genius to surface among women during the past two centuries" (p. 117). Born in Moscow, she entered into a nominal marriage with the paleontologist Vladimir Kovalevsky in 1868 in order to gain the freedom of travel needed to pursue advanced mathematical studies in Europe. International acclaim came to Kovalevsky only near the end of her brief life: in 1888 she received the famous *Prix Bordin* of the French Academy of Sciences and the following year became the first woman Corresponding Member of the Russian Academy of Sciences. It was in 1889, as well, that she was appointed Professor of Mathematics at the University of Stockholm. A brilliant student of infinite series and the application of techniques of analysis to mathematical physics, Kovalevsky was also a gifted writer whose literary output, which included two novels and a memoir of her childhood, centered on the theme of women's rights. Her life and work are discussed by Osen (pp. 117–40) and also by E. T. Bell in *Men of Mathematics* (New York: Simon & Schuster, 1965), pp. 423ff.

2. It was Bereney who, together with Alice Balint's sister, Olga Szekely-Kovacs, sketched the famous caricatures of the first- and second-generation analysts who attended the international psychoanalytic congress in Salzburg in 1924. The sketches were

published as *Karikaturen* (Leipzig: International Psychoanalytischer Verlag, 1924) and reprinted as *Caricatures of 88 Pioneers in Psychoanalysis Drawn from Life at the Eighth International Psychoanalytic Congress* (New York: Basic Books, 1954).

3. Hollós's book, *Hinter der gelben Mauer,* essentially "an appeal to adjust society to the world of the 'insane'" (Kurt Eissler, *Talent and Genius: The Fictitious Case of Tausk contra Freud* [New York: Quadrangle, 1971], p. 318), was published in Hungarian and German in 1927. The letter to which Dr. Mahler calls attention is dated October 4, 1928, and the passage that she paraphrases reads as follows: "Despite my unqualified recognition of the warmth of your feeling, of your comprehension and of the direction in which you are moving, I nevertheless found myself in a sort of opposition which did not become readily understandable to me. At last I admitted to myself that it came from the fact that I do not like these patients, that I am annoyed with them, that I feel them to be so far distant from me and from everything human. A curious sort of intolerance, which surely makes me unfit to be a psychiatrist." Max Schur (*The Id and the Regulatory Principles of Mental Functioning* [New York: International Universities Press, 1966], p. 21f.) was the first to print the complete letter, including the German text, though I quote here the translation by Harold Collins utilized by Eissler (*Talent and Genius,* p. 319).

Chapter 2 Medical Training Between the Wars

1. The "Swedish researcher" whose identity Dr. Mahler could not recollect in the interview covering this period was undoubtedly R. Fåhraeus. In the text, the apposite phrase "or one of his close associates" reflects Dr. Mahler's own uncertainty as to whether she was hired by Fåhraeus himself or one of his associates. In a 1980 interview with Doris Nagel, she reminisces as follows: "I was engaged by a Swedish person— I don't know whether he was the original introducer of the sedimentation rate studies or somebody close to him—to do research with him. . . . " In any event, the sedimentation rate was adopted as a laboratory technique after Fåhraeus published two papers, one in 1918 describing its application in pregnancy, and a better known paper in 1921 (*Acta Med. Scand.,* 55:1) relating it to many other factors. Fåhraeus's work is cited in

John B. Miale, *Laboratory Medicine: Hematology,* 5th ed. (St. Louis, MI: C. V. Mosby, 1977).

2. Emil Feer, *Lehrbuch der Kinderheilkunde.* (Jena: Gustav Fischer, 1911). Von Pirquet, with whom Dr. Mahler subsequently worked in Vienna, contributed the chapters dealing with diseases of the respiratory organs and with tuberculosis to this same textbook. See Richard Wagner, *Clemens von Pirquet: His Life and Work* (Baltimore, MD: Johns Hopkins Press, 1968), p. 94.

3. Dr. Peter Blos informs me that his father, Edwin Blos, was at the time a member of the *Freie wissenschaftliche Studenten Vereinigung* (Union of Free Scientific Students). From its inception during the latter part of the nineteenth century, this liberal student organization opposed pan-Germanism, and the racial discrimination it entailed, at German universities. This goal gained formal expression in the organization's opposition to all duelling fraternities (*Schlagende Verbindungen*) at the universities.

Chapter 3   From Pediatrics to Child Psychiatry

1. We are fortunate to have a scholarly study of von Pirquet, focusing on the very period that is the subject of Dr. Mahler's reminiscences, Richard Wagner's *Clemens von Pirquet: His Life and Work* (Baltimore, MD: Johns Hopkins Press, 1968). The reader interested in exploring the personalities, events, and research projects herein recounted may consult Wagner's informative study.

2. Here is Wagner's useful summary (p. 179) of von Pirquet's tonsil research, which mentions, without naming, Dr. Mahler: "When von Pirquet became director of the *Kinderklinik,* he was horrified at the routine and indiscriminate removal of tonsils, and he dealt with the problem in his characteristic way. He assigned to an intern [i.e., to Dr. Mahler] the task of assessing the size of tonsils of a statistically significant number of normal children during each year of childhood. Analysis of figures based on 5,670 normal children disclosed a peak distribution of enlarged tonsils at the age of four years (infantile hypertrophy) and another at about the tenth year (puerile hypertrophy). Comparison showed that the peak ages for tonsillectomy at the ear, nose, and throat clinic coincided with the peaks for

hypertrophy. Additional information from the English statistics for 4,587 deaths from tonsillitis in the years 1911 to 1920 showed a peak of deaths at four years of age but not at ten years. It thus became clear to von Pirquet that the tonsillar hypertrophy which occurred at four years and ten years of age was a physiological phenomenon which was being interfered with regardless of any real clinical necessity for surgery. After the age of ten years, natural involution of the lymphoid tissue occurs in any case.

"On the basis of such clear-cut findings, von Pirquet immediately discontinued routine tonsillectomy. He allowed the procedure to be carried out only when it was strongly indicated, as when the tonsils were so large that they touched in the midline and interfered with breathing and swallowing, or when there was recurrent infection of the middle ear or deafness. The policy which he advocated has become standard pediatric practice in the United States, but it was not generally accepted here until the last ten or fifteen years." Wagner provides the reference to the publication in which von Pirquet presented his findings: "Hypertrophia tonsillarum infantilis et puerilis," *Zeitschrift für Kinderheilkunde,* 39:372, 1925.

3. Wagner devotes two chapters (pp. 121–62) to the "Pirquet system of nutrition," which was based on an index of nutritional status derived from anthropocentric comparisons of sitting height and weight. The term *nem,* incidentally, is the acronym of *n*utritional *e*quivalent of *m*ilk (p. 134).

4. Aichhorn, a former grade school teacher in the Vienna school system, began his counseling work with delinquent children immediately after World War I. In December 1918, he and several colleagues administered a home for delinquent boys established by the city of Vienna at the former refugee camp at Ober-Hollabrunn. It was in this residential context that he resolved to apply psychoanalysis to the treatment of delinquency. His imaginative therapeutic strategies, discussed by Dr. Mahler below, are recorded in *Wayward Youth* (1925; trans. 1963) and the collection of papers edited by O. Fleischmann, P. Kramer, and H. Ross, *Delinquency and Child Guidance: Selected Papers of August Aichhorn* (New York: International Universities Press, 1964). Brief biographical sketches of Aichhorn have been provided by K. Eissler (in *Searchlights on Delinquency: New Psychoanalytic Studies* [New York: International Universities Press, 1949],

pp. ix–xiii) and A. Freud ("Obituary, August Aichhorn," *International Journal of Psycho-Analysis,* 32:51–56, 1951). For a general consideration of Aichhorn in the context of the postwar Viennese educational reforms and a critical assessment of his counseling work with delinquent children during this time, see P. E. Stepansky, *In Freud's Shadow: Adler in Context* (Hillsdale, NJ: The Analytic Press, 1983) pp. 211ff.

5. Wagner is considerably more positive about Lazar's department, which he views as "a daring experiment" deriving from von Pirquet's interest in psychiatry. Of course, Wagner does not discuss the actual treatment administered to children in the department, much less the routine surgical interventions that Dr. Mahler found so upsetting: "In his opening lecture in Vienna, von Pirquet proposed a psychiatric ward for children. Soon thereafter what he termed a ward for corrective education [what Dr. Mahler calls a 'department of remedial education'] was added to the *Kinderklinik.* The director of the ward, Professor Erwin Lazar, was a pediatrician who had specialized in psychiatry and served as psychiatric adviser to the city's juvenile court. His staff consisted of an assistant and several nurses who had received specialized training in psychometric techniques. Lazar was a pioneer in this field, and the venture which he and von Pirquet undertook requried a good deal of courage. Freud's followers were found chiefly among a few lay groups; the more conservative medical profession had not accepted his views on psychoanalysis, nor had the general public. . . . Neither Lazar nor von Pirquet was hostile to Freud's concept.

"Von Pirquet had deep interest in the work Lazar was doing and never failed to listen patiently to the long histories of patients on his ward during morning rounds. Many of the children were referred by the police or juvenile court because of behavioral problems. They were first given medical and psychiatric evaluations, followed by a period of careful observation. Occasionally the mental abnormality was found to be the result of transitory somatic disease. Sometimes there were developmental or educational errors which could be corrected by adequate training. In certain instances, transferral to an institution for mentally retarded children or to a reform school was necessary. Often the child was normal but had suffered emotional trauma because of unjust treatment by a parent—an hysterical mother or an alcoholic father. In each case, treatment was directed toward alleviation of the underlying cause. Von Pirquet was particularly interested in the deviation from normal behavior resulting from organic brain disease, such as the traits of delinquency that develop after encephalitis. One of his favorite speculations was that sudden changes in the blood supply to the brain might cause oscillations in an individual's psychological state" (pp. 110–111).

Chapter 4   Becoming a Psychoanalyst in Vienna

1. W. Hoffer, "Mouth, Hand, and Ego-Integration," *The Psychoanalytic Study of the Child,* 3/4:49–56, 1949; "Development of the Body Ego," *The Psychoanalytic Study of the Child,* 5:18–23, 1950; "Oral Aggressiveness and Ego Development," *International Journal of Psycho-Analysis,* 31:156–60, 1950.

2. It should be noted that Dr. Mahler provided in her will for the transportation of Paul Mahler's ashes with her own ashes for burial in the Jewish Cemetery in Sopron, Hungary.

3. "During the thirties, Editha gave birth to two children, both girls. . . . During the infancy and early years of our older daughter, Dr. Margret Schönberger was our pediatrician. Dr. Schönberger, who published under her married name, Mahler, received world-wide recognition for her studies of early childhood development. As pediatrician for our daughter, she insisted that the baby be weighed before and after every breastfeeding to determine the exact quantity of nourishment taken, a procedure not uncommon during the period of breastfeeding. She was very conscientious and exacting, and always saw the child on housecalls; our daughter thrived under her care. When our second daughter was born three years after the first, Dr. Schönberger was too occupied with her analytic work, and we had to change to another pediatrician." Richard F. Sterba, *Reminiscences of a Viennese Psychoanalyst* (Detroit, MI: Wayne State University Press, 1982), p. 96.

4. This claim, and the passage that follows, only appears to contradict Dr. Mahler's earlier remarks (p. 69) about the flexible and nondoctrinaire attitude toward "neutrality" adopted by Viennese training analysts of the time. The salient point, of course, is that her remarks about neutrality as a mere "guideline" were intended to characterize *training* analyses whereas the current discussion pertains to *therapeutic* analyses.

Chapter 5 Sea Change

1. I can locate no posthumous publication of Abraham's dealing expressly with masturbation. Given the context of Dr. Mahler's reminiscence (i.e., her conversations with Hedwig Abraham about the Abrahams' daughter, Hilda), it may be that Mrs. Abraham shared with her Abraham's brief handwritten log of Hilda's childhood symptoms and of several conversations he had with her. This log was published in the *International Review of Psycho-Analysis* in 1974 (volume 1, pp. 5–14) under the title "Little Hilda: Daydreams and a Symptom in a Seven-Year-Old Girl." This paper contains the following passage: "She [Hilda] has confessed that she masturbates and once was even caught doing so. I told her at the time that she should not go on doing it, as she would then always lie in bed at night and stay awake, and would be tired the next morning and not be as fresh and lively as the other children at school" (p. 6). Hardly a "punitive" admonition, but Dr. Mahler may be hearkening back to Mrs. Abraham's disclosures to her that followed, and presumably elaborated upon, the subject matter of Abraham's log.

Chapter 6 First Years in America

1. Herman Nunberg, who arrived in New York in the fall of 1934, recounts an equally inhospitable reception by the senior New York analysts. His initial application for membership in the New York Psychoanalytic Society was rejected because he refused to give up his membership in the Vienna Psychoanalytic Society. Following Hitler's occupation of Austria in 1938, he reapplied for membership, "justifying that move by the fact that, since the Vienna society had been dissolved, the question of my dual membership no longer existed. To my puzzlement, however, my application was unanimously rejected, as I was notified in a letter signed by Dr. Adolf Stern, then chairman of the Educational Committee. I was informed that while I would be permitted to complete the current training analyses and supervisions, no training analyses or supervisions of mine would be recognized thereafter. Soon I learned privately that it had been Sandor Rado who pushed through this decision of the Educational Committee—the same Rado who, as all members of the Educational Committee must have

known, had moved farther and farther away from psychoanalysis, had even given up its basic tenets and yet still called himself a psychoanalyst." See Herman Nunberg, *Memoirs: Recollections, Ideas, Reflections* (New York: Psychoanalytic Research and Development Fund, 1969), pp. 64–65.

2. It should be reiterated that a good many analysts from New York and elsewhere in the country exerted themselves to obtain the affidavits that enabled their European colleagues to come to the United States in the first place.

3. "Pseudoimbecility: A Magic Cap of Invisibility," *Psychoanalytic Quarterly*, 11:149–64, 1942. Reprinted in *Selected Papers of Margaret S. Mahler*, vol. I, pp. 3–16.

4. M. S. Mahler and L. Rangell, "A Psychosomatic Study of Maladie des Tics (Gilles de la Tourette's disease)," *Psychiatric Quarterly*, 17:579–603, 1943.

5. The expression Dr. Mahler has in mind is undoubtedly "predispositional deficiency." In *On Human Symbiosis and the Vicissitudes of Individuation* (New York: International Universities Press, 1968), she writes as follows: ". . . it must be abundantly clear that I regard the issue of nature-nurture a moot one. Looking at autistic and symbiotic psychotic children, one cannot help but feel that the primary etiology of psychosis in children, the psychotic child's primary defect in being able to utilize (to perceive) the catalyzing mothering agent for homeostasis, is inborn, constitutional, and probably hereditary, or else acquired very early in the very first days or weeks of extrauterine life. In other words, there seems to be a predispositional deficiency (N. D. C. Lewis)" (pp. 47–48).

6. M. S. Mahler and J. A. Luke, "Outcome of the Tic Syndrome," *Journal of Nervous and Mental Disease*, 103:433–45, 1946. Reprinted in *The Selected Papers of Margaret S. Mahler*, vol. I, pp. 89–106.

7. M. S. Mahler, J. R. Ross, Jr., and Z. De Fries, "Clinical Studies in Benign and Malignant Cases of Childhood Psychosis (Schizophrenia-like)," *American Journal of Orthopsychiatry*, 19 : 295–305, 1949.

8. The special permit for Dr. Mahler's parents was obtained by the Hebrew Immigrant Aid Society (HIAS).

9. W. Kornfeld and M. Schönberger, "Untersuchungen zur

Frage der sexuellen Differenzierung einiger Körpermasse und Proportionen bei 7 jährigen Kindern" [Investigations into the Question of the Sexual Differentiation of Some Body Measurements and Proportions in 7-Year-Old Children], *Zeitschrift für Kinderheilkunde*, 47:676–701, 1929.

10. M. S. Mahler, "Discussion of 'Mother Types Encountered in Child Guidance Clinics,' by J. Silberpfennig," *American Journal of Orthopsychiatry*, 11:484, 1941; M. S. Mahler, "Schizophrenia in Childhood," *Nervous Child*, 1:137–50, 1941, abstracted in the *Psychoanalytic Quarterly*, 13:131–33, 1944.

11. M. S. Mahler and J. Silberpfennig, "Der Rorschachsche Formdeutversuch als Hilfsmittel zum Verständnis der Psychologie Hirnkranker" [Rorschach Interpretation as an Aid in Understanding the Psychology of the Brain-Damaged], *Schweizer Archiv für Neurologie und Psychiatrie*, 40:302–27, 1938.

Chapter 7 Professional Fulfillment

1. M. S. Mahler and M. Furer, "Observations on Research Regarding the 'Symbiotic Syndrome' of Infantile Psychosis," *Psychoanalytic Quarterly*, 29:317–27, 1960. Reprinted in *The Selected Papers of Margaret S. Mahler*, vol. I, pp. 223–32.

2. Dr. Furer recollects that the pilot study was conducted in 1962–63. See F. Pine and M. Furer, "Studies of the Separation-Individuation Phase: A Methodological Overview," *The Psychoanalytic Study of the Child*, 18:325–42, 1963.

3. M. S. Mahler and B. J. Gosliner, "On Symbiotic Child Psychosis: Genetic, Dynamic, and Restitutive Aspects," *The Psychoanalytic Study of the Child*, 10:195–212, 1955. Reprinted in *The Selected Papers of Margaret S. Mahler*, vol. I, pp. 109–29.

Epilogue

1. M. S. Mahler, "Pseudoimbecility: A Magic Cap of Invisibility," *Psychoanalytic Quarterly*, 11:149–64, 1942; M. S. Mahler, "'Les Enfants Terribles,'" in *Searchlights on Delinquency*, ed. K. R. Eissler (New York: International Universities Press,

1949), pp. 77–89. Both papers are reprinted in *The Selected Papers of Margaret S. Mahler,* vol. I, pp. 3–16 and 17–33.

2. Louise J. Kaplan, *Oneness and Separateness: From Infant to Individual* (New York: Simon & Schuster, 1978).

Afterword

1. The information that follows about Margaret Mahler's relation to Judaism, including her early experiences of anti-Semitism and the fate of her family members during the Holocaust, was conveyed to me by Bernard Fischman, Esq. Mr. Fischman mentioned these particulars in his funeral eulogy for Dr. Mahler of October 6, 1985.

2. These data about the fate of the Jewish residents of Sopron following the German occupation of March–April 1944 were obtained by Mrs. Bernice Apter, who attended the burial of Dr. Mahler's ashes in Sopron on August 1, 1986.

3. The preface to the Hebrew translation of *Totem and Taboo* is found in *The Standard Edition of the Complete Psychological Works of Sigmund Freud,* trans. and ed. James Strachey et al. (London: Hogarth Press, 1953–64), vol. 13, p. xv.

Index